DATE DUE

PRINTED IN U.S.A.

MELTDOWN

EARTHQUAKE, TSUNAMI, AND NUCLEAR DISASTER IN FUKUSHIMA

DEIRDRE LANGELAND

Roaring Brook Press
New York

A note on magnitude and terminology: The earthquake and tsunami event that occurred off the northeast coast of Japan on March 11, 2011, is commonly called by several different names. The Japan Meteorological Agency originally referred to it as the 2011 Off the Pacific Coast of Tohoku Earthquake and later as the Great East Japan Earthquake. It is often listed as the Tohoku-Oki Earthquake as well. For the purpose of this book, I have called it by the name used by the U.S. Geological Survey (USGS) and the U.S. National Oceanographic and Atmospheric Administration: the Great Tohoku Earthquake. The reported magnitude of the event also varies by source, but was revised upward to 9.1 by the USGS in November 2016.

On the scale used by seismologists to measure large earthquakes, the Moment Magnitude Scale, each jump in magnitude is an increase in energy released of thirty-two times, resulting in an increase of ten times in the amplitude of the seismic waves generated by the event. The terms "hypocenter" and "subduction fault," used herein, are synonymous with the terms "focus" and "megathrust," respectively.

Published by Roaring Brook Press
Roaring Brook Press is a division of Holtzbrinck Publishing Holdings Limited Partnership
120 Broadway, New York, NY 10271 • mackids.com

ISBN 978-1-62672-700-7
Library of Congress Control Number 2020912214

Our books may be purchased in bulk for promotional, educational, or business use. Please contact your local bookseller or the Macmillan Corporate and Premium Sales Department at (800) 221-7945 ext. 5442 or by email at MacmillanSpecialMarkets@macmillan.com.

First edition, 2021
Book design by Jen Keenan
Printed in China by Toppan Leefung Printing Ltd., Dongguan City, Guangdong Province

1 3 5 7 9 10 8 6 4 2

For my mother, Ricky Langeland, who taught me how to be curious, do my research, and think like a scientist.

CONTENTS

Most of the area of Japan is made up of four major islands. The largest of these, Honshu, is divided into five distinct regions. The northernmost, the area most affected by the March 11, 2011, earthquake, is known as Tohoku (shown here in dark blue).

PREFACE

Fukushima. To people all around the world, the name has come to mean one thing: nuclear disaster. They remember several long weeks in March 2011 when they turned on the news every day and saw thick smoke billowing from nuclear reactors, carrying potentially deadly radiation into the environment.

In reality, Fukushima is a prefecture in Japan—a government district similar to a state in America. It's the southernmost prefecture in the Tohoku region, an area of about 25,000 square miles that is famous for its remote beauty. Dense forests and volcanic peaks define the landscape. Fog drifting in from the northern Pacific Ocean blankets its rice paddies, apple orchards, and cattle farms. Before the disaster, Fukushima was known as a lush farming area that supplied produce, dairy products, and seafood to the rest of Japan. But in the space of a few days, all of that changed.

Roughly midway along the Fukushima coast, six nuclear reactors were lined up in a neat row along the shore. Owned by the Tokyo Electric Power Company, or TEPCO, they were part of the Fukushima Daiichi power plant. (*Dai-ichi* means "one" in Japanese. A second power plant, called Fukushima Daini, meaning "two," was located about 6 miles down the shore.)

On March 11, 2011, the plants were hit by a one-two punch: First, there was the earthquake, the strongest ever measured in Japan. Then came the tsunami, an inescapable wall of water that killed tens of thousands. Together, they crippled the reactors at Fukushima Daiichi, setting off a chain of events that threatened the safety of millions.

—ᴧ—

Like most disasters, the Great Tohoku Earthquake and tsunami came with little warning. There had been foreshocks, smaller earthquakes that shook the countryside for days before the main event, but there's nothing unusual about earthquakes in Japan. On average, Japan experiences about two thousand earthquakes that are strong enough to be felt every year. In real time, it's impossible to know whether an earthquake is its own event or a precursor of something bigger on the way. Only afterward, once the Big One has come and gone, can seismologists go back and see the pattern that led up to it. And so, the millions of residents of Tohoku went about their business that afternoon in March as they had on all of the others before.

That was certainly true for Ryoichi Usuzawa, a sixty-two-year-old grandfather with salt-and-pepper hair who was working from his home in the town of Otsuchi. He was pleased with himself because he had just finished writing a report and was binding it into a folder and adding tabs. His wife was downstairs with the family dog, a Shiba Inu named Taro. It seemed like a pretty ordinary Friday afternoon, and Ryoichi was happy to be wrapping up the week's work.

But what happened next was anything but ordinary. "Suddenly, there was a[n] . . . enormous earthquake," he later told a journalist. "Nothing like what we'd experienced in the past—a truly terrifying quake. It made me wonder if our house would collapse; if I might die. The printer, computer, bookshelf, records—everything came tumbling down. I couldn't move a step."

When the shaking stopped, just a little past 2:50 P.M., Ryoichi did what he had probably done after the hundreds of smaller earthquakes that had shaken his house in the past: He began to clean up the mess. Even when his wife told him there was a tsunami warning, he didn't think it was a serious threat. After all, his family had lived there for decades and the water had never reached their land. For the next half hour, he straightened up and tried to fix the television as his sons, his daughter-in-law, and a grandchild gathered outside the house. He tried to calm his nerves, which had been jangled by the unusually strong earthquake.

Then he heard his wife shouting: "Oto-San, run from the tsunami!"

—∿—

Like hundreds of thousands of others who lived along the coast of Tohoku, Ryoichi was at the start of what would be a long, terrifying ordeal. By nightfall, much of his hometown, including his own house, would be swallowed by waves.

But Ryoichi had no way of knowing that. He only knew that his wife's last words as she ran for safety were "Look after Taro!" So he headed up the stairs, in the direction he had last seen the dog going.

Moments later, muddy water surged up the stairs after him.

DAY 1

earthquake

Friday, March 11, 2011, 2:46 P.M.

```
┌─ Reactor Status ─────────────────────────────────┐
│    Reactor 1: Fully operational                   │
│    Reactor 2: Fully operational                   │
│    Reactor 3: Fully operational                   │
│    Reactor 4: Shut down for inspection            │
│    Reactor 5: Shut down for inspection            │
│    Reactor 6: Shut down for inspection            │
└───────────────────────────────────────────────────┘
```

Standing on Earth, it's difficult to appreciate its movement. The entire planet spins on its axis at more than 1,000 miles per hour (mph) and hurtles along its orbit through space at 66,660 mph. It's no wonder, then, that those of us sitting on its surface hardly notice the slow creep of its tectonic plates. But miles beneath the soil and sand, the mountains and oceans, Earth's lithosphere is broken into a clumsy jigsaw puzzle of rock. The puzzle pieces, called tectonic plates, sit on the asthenosphere, a layer of Earth that shifts and flows.

Rocks in the asthenosphere are under so much pressure that they move in and out of solid form—sometimes they are solid rocks, sometimes liquid magma. Resting on top of this constantly changing layer, the plates creep over, under, and past each other at a rate so slow it would make a snail blush.

More than anything else, Japan has been shaped by the push and pull of plate tectonics. Just off its east coast, deep beneath the seafloor, giant chunks of Earth's lithosphere and crust are being sucked beneath the country in a process called subduction. Rock from the subducting plates turns to magma when it reaches the mantle, creating hot spots that, over millennia, melt through the crust and break through as lava, forming volcanoes. That up-welling magma is responsible for the breathtaking mountainous landscape of Japan, and those subducting plates cause most of the earthquakes that shake the country.

Japan is an archipelago, a cluster of islands that sit on a particularly active spot in the tectonic neighborhood, where a thin finger of the North American Plate extends down between the

Mount Fuji, Japan's tallest peak, is one of more than a hundred active volcanoes in the country.

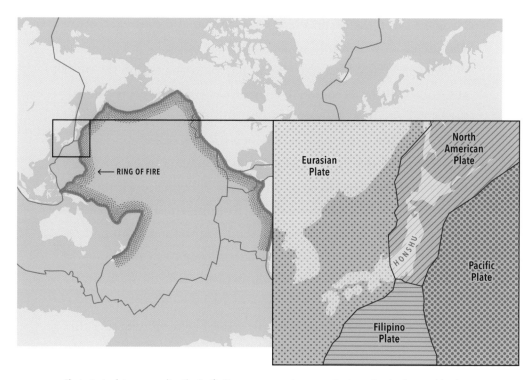

The tectonic plates surrounding the Pacific Ocean are converging, or moving toward each other, resulting in a rough arc of subduction faults around the edge of the ocean. Because these faults produce volcanic activity, the arc has become known as the Ring of Fire. On the other side of the world, beneath the Atlantic Ocean, the tectonic plates are moving apart, or diverging, which creates a more stable seismic environment.

Eurasian and Pacific Plates. The largest of the islands, Honshu, is in an especially precarious position, straddling the boundary between the Eurasian and North American Plates. To the east of the island, the North American and Pacific Plates meet in a section of the seafloor called the Japan Trench. There, the Pacific Plate slides beneath the North American Plate in what's known as a subduction fault.

It sounds harmless enough, and even more so when you realize that the Pacific Plate creeps westward at only about three and a half inches per year. But tectonic plates don't slide smoothly—they stick. And on a scale as large as a tectonic plate, a little bit of motion combined with a lot of stickiness can build up an enormous amount of energy.

As the Pacific Plate slides beneath the North American Plate, it catches the North American Plate's edge. Over time, the movement of the Pacific Plate pulls the North American Plate downward, like the bucket of a catapult that is being readied

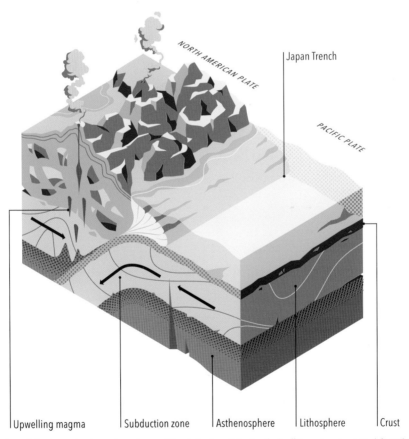

NORTH AMERICAN PLATE

Japan Trench

PACIFIC PLATE

| Upwelling magma | Subduction zone | Asthenosphere | Lithosphere | Crust

Japan's landscape has been shaped over millennia by the subduction fault off its eastern coast. Rock from the subducting plate melts when it reaches the mantle, creating hot spots of magma.

to fire. The upper plate begins to bend, curving at the fault and forming a deep ocean trench. Tension builds between the two. Potential energy grows. When the potential energy in the fault becomes greater than the force, called friction, that holds the plates together, the top plate breaks free and springs upward. The subducting plate surges forward. The catapult has been released. The strength of the resulting earthquake depends on how much energy has built up in the fault before it budges, how much of the fault slips, and how far it moves.

The many faults surrounding Japan are constantly slipping. In fact, the country experiences a tremor somewhere within its borders every five minutes or so. Most of those are too small for humans to feel. Of the two thousand or so each year that are strong enough to be felt, most are small tremors, which do little more than rattle dishes and set off car alarms. But the Great Tohoku Earthquake, as it came to be known, was far more powerful than any that had been measured in Japan before.

Scientists rate the strength of an earthquake using the moment magnitude scale, a system that gauges the amount of energy released by the quake and assigns it a number. Each number on the scale is ten times more powerful than the one before it. An earthquake that rates a 5 on the scale is strong enough to be felt by everyone, rattling dishes and waking sleepers in their beds. An earthquake that rates a 6 is ten times more powerful than a 5. A 7 is 100 times more powerful than a 5, toppling furniture and shaking loose plaster and bricks in older buildings. The Tohoku quake was measured at 9.1.

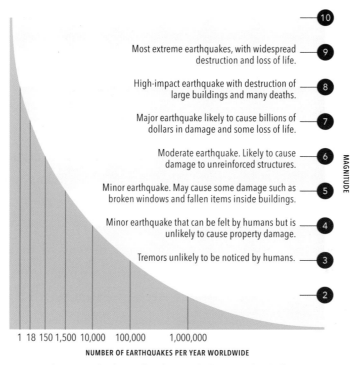

10

Most extreme earthquakes, with widespread destruction and loss of life. — 9

High-impact earthquake with destruction of large buildings and many deaths. — 8

Major earthquake likely to cause billions of dollars in damage and some loss of life. — 7

Moderate earthquake. Likely to cause damage to unreinforced structures. — 6

Minor earthquake. May cause some damage such as broken windows and fallen items inside buildings. — 5

Minor earthquake that can be felt by humans but is unlikely to cause property damage. — 4

Tremors unlikely to be noticed by humans. — 3

2

MAGNITUDE

1 18 150 1,500 10,000   100,000   1,000,000

NUMBER OF EARTHQUAKES PER YEAR WORLDWIDE

Determining the magnitude of an earthquake is a tricky business. After the fact, seismologists study measurements of the ground's movement taken by seismographs and evaluate the damage done by the quake to decide what magnitude to assign to the event.

Before 2011, most scientists believed that the Japan Trench could not produce an earthquake stronger than magnitude 7.5. That's because it's not a very sticky fault—it moves forward pretty smoothly, without building up too much friction between the plates. And less sticking means that less potential energy builds up in the fault.

But in the end, it was the fault's slipperiness that proved the scientific predictions wrong. The upper plate lurched forward on March 9, causing a magnitude 7.2 earthquake—on its own a major event. Three more large quakes, each larger than magnitude 6, followed that same day. Then the fault ruptured again.

At 2:46 P.M. on March 11, an area of the North American Plate about 190 miles long broke free from the Pacific Plate. The fault was packed with slippery clay, which acted like the water on a slip-and-slide, allowing the Pacific Plate to leap more than 160 feet westward—farther than anyone had thought it could go. Energy surged from the rupture like a bomb blast, racing toward the shore at nearly 4 miles per second.

In Japan, March marks the end of the school year. On that Friday afternoon, many kids were nearing the end of their last day of classes. Office workers were grinding through afternoon meetings and paperwork. Stores were preparing for the after-noon rush. Then the earthquake sirens sounded. Seconds later, the ground began to shake. Glass shattered, roadways crumbled, and telephone poles toppled.

Three prefectures along the northeastern coast of the island— Iwate, Miyagi, and Fukushima—were closest to the fault and took the hardest hit. In the town of Otsuchi, in Iwate prefec-ture, Ryoichi Usuzawa was rattled at his desk. Nearby, a barber named Seizo Sasaki was in his shop when the quake hit. "First, everything started to sway, slowly and lazily," he later recalled. "Then with a sudden wrench, the quake hit hard."

At first, it seemed like every other earthquake. All over the island of Honshu, people followed emergency guidelines and dropped to the floor, sheltering under desks and tables as they waited for the shaking to stop. Normally, an earthquake lasts for a few seconds, maybe as many as thirty. A big earthquake might go on for a full minute—but not this time. A minute ticked by, and the shaking didn't stop. It got worse. In some places, it lasted for five long minutes.

All over Japan, people began to realize that this was not an average event. "I never experienced such a strong earthquake in my life," a city official from Sendai told a reporter in disbelief that night. "I thought it would stop, but it just kept shaking and shaking, and getting stronger."

Up and down the coast, violent tremors knocked out power and toppled warning towers. Sendai, a large city close to the epicenter, was hit by the full force of the quake, but all of Honshu felt it.

—〰—

The energy that surges from a ruptured fault shakes the earth from crust to core. The movement produces what is known as seismic waves. Most of the shaking that we think of as an earthquake is caused by a category of seismic wave known as surface waves, which roil Earth's crust, taking everything on it for a ride. Of those surface waves, Love waves shake from side to side, while Rayleigh waves roll in circles, creating up-and-down motion at the surface. If you've ever been on a boat as it rocked over ocean swells, you probably have a good idea of what Rayleigh motion feels like. Imagine being vigorously shaken from side to side as the boat is riding over those swells, and you can start to get an idea of what it feels like when Rayleigh and Love waves combine in an earthquake. When that combined motion is in the ground beneath your feet, the effects can be devastating.

In Tokyo, about 180 miles from the epicenter, journalist David McNeill was in a subway station when the earthquake struck.

He later described the rolling motion of the surface waves: "It began not with a jolt, like many quakes, but with an almost lazy undulating rocking motion that slowly built in intensity until the station's roof rattled violently and glass shattered on the platform . . . We stood frozen to the spot, hearts thumping violently, and watching the roof, silently praying it wouldn't fall on top of our heads."

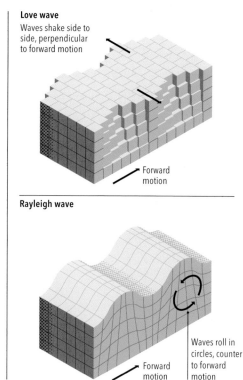

Love wave
Waves shake side to side, perpendicular to forward motion

Forward motion

Rayleigh wave

Waves roll in circles, counter to forward motion

Forward motion

Buildings in the city, designed to withstand earthquakes, bent rather than broke as the ground beneath them rolled. "What was scariest was to look up at the skyscrapers all around," one witness said. "They were swaying like trees in the breeze."

But the subway did not collapse, and the skyscrapers didn't crumble. Even in the midst of such a massive quake, many of Japan's earthquake protection systems worked.

Japan is often called the most earthquake-prepared country in the world. Since an earthquake killed thousands in the city of Kobe in 1995, the nation had spent sixteen years reinforcing bridges,

Customers huddle against a support pole for protection as the ceiling in a bookstore collapses during the Great Tohoku Earthquake.

reconstructing old buildings with earthquake-resistant technology, and creating earthquake warning systems. New buildings in Japan are designed to rock and flex rather than break, helping them weather strong quakes. But in 2011, it may have been the warning systems that saved the most lives.

When a fault ruptures, the energy travels in four kinds of seismic waves. While Love and Rayleigh waves roil Earth's surface and secondary waves shake solid rock deep within the planet, primary waves travel through Earth's mantle and core, causing little damage on the surface. Each kind of wave moves at a different speed, and those different speeds make it possible for some very clever equipment to detect an earthquake before it can be felt by humans.

Primary waves, or P waves, travel very fast—as fast as 3.7 miles per second through Earth's crust and 8 miles per second through the core. When earthquake monitoring stations register P waves, they trip early warning sirens, giving people crucial time to turn off motors, stop surgeries, and pull cars to the side of the road before the surface waves arrive. The warnings trigger automated safety systems, forcing elevators to come to a halt and open their doors. Subway trains slow to a stop. For towns and cities close to the epicenter of the Great Tohoku Earthquake, the warning came fifteen seconds before the tremors. That might not sound like a long time, but it was enough to keep cars and trains from crashing, prevent people from being trapped in elevators, and give others time to scramble to cover.

The early warning system worked perfectly in Fukushima prefecture. When the first seismic waves reached the power plant at Fukushima Daiichi, fail-safe systems shut down the reactors. When the prolonged shaking knocked out power lines, backup generators clicked on to run the plant's instrument panels and keep critical coolant moving through the reactors.

In the end, most of the severe damage caused by the quake was the result of liquefaction. Cities built near major bodies of water often create new land by dumping soil and rubble, called landfill, into bays and ocean inlets. Under normal conditions, this reclaimed land is a perfectly stable base for buildings and parks. But when an earthquake shakes landfill, it can spell trouble, especially when the surrounding soil is sandy.

Sandy soil can store a lot of water. The grains of sand are stacked haphazardly, with water molecules between them. But when the soil is shaken, the structure holding up the grains

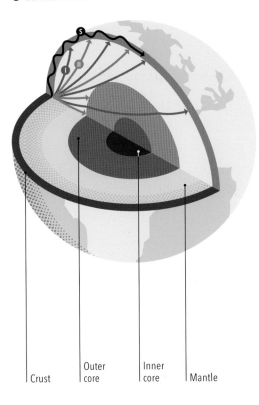

- **P** Primary waves
- **S** Secondary waves
- **S** Surface waves

Crust | Outer core | Inner core | Mantle

The four main types of seismic waves each have distinct characteristics. Primary waves and secondary waves are body waves–they travel through the layers of the Earth beneath the crust. Primary waves are the only kind that can travel through both solid rock and molten lava. They radiate through Earth's mantle and core, having little effect on Earth's surface. Secondary waves move through the solid rock of the mantle, but cannot penetrate the molten iron outer core. They cause some damage to the land above. Love and Rayleigh waves are surface waves, and produce most of the shaking felt during an earthquake.

collapses, causing water from below to rise toward the surface. Each shake makes more grains sink and more water rise, building up water pressure in the soil. When the pressure is great enough, the ground begins to move like a liquid. When that ground is underneath a building or a road, the result can be catastrophic.

A woman named Yukari Kurosawa was working at a hospital in Otsuchi when the quake struck. Afterward, she described the effects of liquefaction—indoors and out. "Suddenly everything started to shake," she remembered. "Even the heavy desk, which always took so much effort for us to move, was jigging up and down like a toy." When a coworker shouted at her to get out of the building, she moved to the parking lot, where the ground beneath the pavement had liquefied. "Outside, the asphalt was rolling and heaving. 'Asphalt waves,' I thought when I saw it."

All around Japan, sections of parking lot and road seemed to turn to liquid. The metal tubes lining manholes popped out of the pavement as the ground around them sank and settled. In Chiba City, where parkland had been created on landfill dumped into Tokyo Bay, the sidewalks rippled like fabric. The ground

Light structures like this bus stop were shaken apart by the quake.

sloshed and swayed, and water spurted rhythmically from the lawn, sounding like waves lapping on a shore.

Just outside of Chiba, at a refinery owned by Cosmo Oil, a huge storage tank had been filled with water—instead of the lighter natural gas it was meant to hold—for inspection. Braces reinforcing the legs of the overburdened tank snapped during the heavy shaking of the earthquake. About a half hour later, the tank's legs buckled and broke, sending it crashing into a pipeline carrying fuel. As a mixure of propane and butane poured from the broken pipe, flames spread across it, crawling along the ground until they reached a nearby fuel tank. It exploded, spreading the fire to another tank, and another, and another. It would be ten days before firefighters were able to put the fire out completely.

The tank collapse at the Cosmo Oil refinery caused a fire that raged for more than a week after the earthquake.

In Fukushima prefecture, the shaking rattled Sukagawa, a town about 40 miles from the coast. It sent the Fujinuma Dam sliding nearly 15 feet downhill, and water from the reservoir behind it began to spill over its top. About twenty minutes after the earthquake, the water pouring over the dam caused it to collapse entirely, flooding nearby homes and killing eight people.

But despite these tragedies, the most remarkable thing about the Great Tohoku Earthquake was how well the Japanese system worked. When the shaking subsided, about 26,600 houses had been destroyed, and 1,476 people were dead. In comparison, the Kobe Earthquake of 1995, with a magnitude of 6.8, had killed 6,308 people. The Tohoku quake, at magnitude 9.1, was more than 100 times more powerful.

Such a massive quake could have caused damage much, much worse. By magnitude-9 standards, the country had fared well.

That was before the tsunami.

tsunami

Friday, March 11, 2011

Reactor Status
Reactor 1: Scrammed
Reactor 2: Scrammed
Reactor 3: Scrammed
Reactor 4: Shut down for inspection
Reactor 5: Shut down for inspection
Reactor 6: Shut down for inspection

After the earthquake, people all over Japan were in shock. They began to take stock of the damage, checking in with classmates, family members, and neighbors. The violent shaking had shattered glass, fragmented roads, toppled telephone poles, collapsed bus shelters and sheds. Indoors, rooms that had been neat and orderly five minutes earlier looked like they had been ransacked. Bookshelves and dressers had capsized, scattering their contents everywhere.

But it wasn't just furniture and buildings that had shifted—when the Japan Trench ruptured, the shape of the entire planet changed. A NASA scientist later calculated that the movement of rock, magma, and soil had shifted Earth's center of gravity, causing the planet to spin a microsecond faster. (A microsecond is one millionth of a second.) The Pacific Plate had slid westward, but the North American Plate had also jumped. When the quake was over, parts of the island of Honshu were as much as 13 feet farther east than when it began.

Honshu didn't move. It *stretched*. For thousands of years, the North American Plate, caught between the Pacific and Eurasian Plates, had been squeezed by the two larger plates. It had compressed, gradually squashing into a smaller space. But it had also bowed, curving and collapsing a little like a kitchen sponge when you squeeze it between your thumb and fingers. As the Pacific Plate slipped westward, the North American Plate sprang back toward its original shape. This left parts of the island's east coast farther from its western edge. The elevation of this area changed, too. As the arch flattened, as much as 250 miles of coastline—roughly equal to the distance from New York City to Washington, D.C.—sank by 2 feet.

At the fault, about 60 miles east of the Honshu coast, 190 miles of seafloor along the edge of the North American Plate leaped upward by about 30 feet. That displaced—pushed away—millions of gallons of water. The water had to go somewhere.

Have you ever dropped a rock into a puddle or a pond? Water splashes up when the rock breaks the surface, and circular ripples spread out from the point where it entered the water. This is an example of displacement on a very small scale. When the rock falls in, it takes up space that used to be occupied by water, so the liquid has to move out of the way. Some of it leaps from the

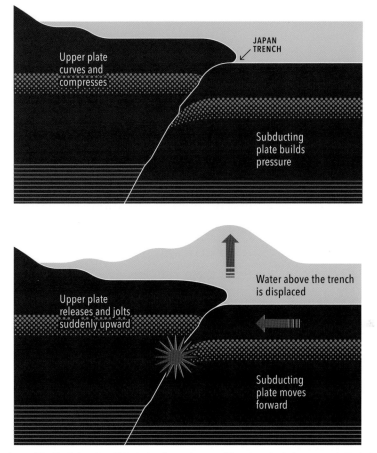

The release of the North American Plate during the quake caused its outer edge to leap upward, displacing the water above it. At the same time, land near the shore flattened, causing a drop of about two feet along the coast.

surface as a splash, and some of it forms a circular ripple, a series of tiny waves radiating from the rock's entry point.

In an earthquake, the effect is similar, but the displacement comes from below. When the seafloor springs up, it shoves millions of gallons of water upward and outward. On the surface, the water creates waves much like the ripple made by the rock. But on this much larger scale, those ripples form a tsunami.

In the open ocean, a tsunami moves incredibly fast—up to 500 miles per hour. The waves are pretty small, usually only a few feet high, and they could be separated in time by as much as an hour. Ships at sea don't notice tsunami waves. As they pass beneath the hull, they feel like any other ocean swells. But unlike most waves, which disturb only the water near the surface, the movement of a tsunami extends all the way to the ocean floor. The entire ocean surges forward at breakneck speed. As the tsunami reaches shallower water near land, it begins to slow down. The shallower the water is, the slower the waves are—but they grow taller.

Imagine an entire classroom of kids walking in line to the playground. Better yet, imagine them running. If the first kid in line stops, or even just slows down dramatically, the kids behind will crash into her. The ones at the back will quickly catch up and run into the ones who have piled up in front. The same thing happens with water. As the front of the wave slows, the water behind it piles on. All that water surging forward needs to go somewhere, so it goes upward. The wave grows taller. Exactly how tall the wave becomes, and how fast it is going when it hits land, depends on the shape of the ocean floor and of the shoreline it is approaching.

If the prospect of a giant wave doesn't sound so bad to you, consider this: 1 cubic yard of water (enough to equal about the size of a washing machine) weighs about 1,700 pounds. Rushing water 6 inches deep is strong enough to sweep adults off their feet. A foot of rushing water can carry away a car. And, although a tsunami near the shore is moving slower than it was at sea, it's still moving faster than a car on a highway, usually about 100 miles per hour. In other words, a tsunami strikes land like a line of Mack trucks moving at top speed.

Like all tsunamis, the waves generated by the Great Tohoku Earthquake traveled across the ocean without slowing down. The

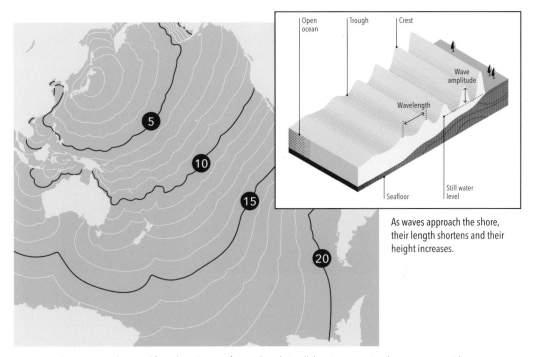

As waves approach the shore, their length shortens and their height increases.

Tsunamis travel outward from the epicenter of an earthquake in all directions, crossing the open ocean until they reach land. The black circles on this chart show the number of hours that elapsed between the time the tsunami was generated and its arrival at different locations around the world.

tsunami would reach Crescent City, California, more than 5,000 miles away, as an 8-foot-high wave almost ten hours later. In eighteen hours, it would hit the Sulzberger Ice Shelf in Antarctica, where it would knock loose an iceberg twice the size of Manhattan. But long before it reached those shores, it would strike Japan.

⎯⌇⎯

Japan has a long history of tsunamis. The word itself—*tsunami*—is Japanese. While tsunamis can occur anywhere in the world, the shape of the coast in the Tohoku region makes them particularly devastating. The northeastern shore of Honshu, often called

On the Sanriku Coast, which extends through Iwate and Miyagi prefectures, the shoreline zigzags in and out like the teeth of a saw.

the Sanriku Coast, zigzags in and out, forming jagged shapes that resemble the teeth of a saw. Rias, riverbeds that have been flooded by the sea, form deep harbors that reach inland, creating channels that can funnel waves. The riverbeds provide a perfect path for a tsunami to flow inland and high up mountainsides.

In the area around Otsuchi, the land alongside those rias flattens out for miles, making it ideal for farming. But when a tsunami comes, that farmland becomes a wide floodplain that is difficult to escape in a hurry.

From an early age, children in Tohoku are taught an evacuation strategy called *tendenko*. Precious time is lost when parents go searching for their children or neighbors stop and check in on each other—or, worse yet, if people are left waiting for help. It may seem ruthless, but the strategy is simple: When a strong earthquake strikes, a tsunami is likely following close behind.

Each person should evacuate separately to a safe place. Do not stop. Do not look for others. If everyone follows *tendenko*, then people can be confident that their children, parents, neighbors, and friends are getting out of harm's way—there will be no need to check on loved ones. Each person is free to evacuate quickly.

That sound advice has rippled through coastal towns for centuries. Misa Koshida, a grandmother in Otsuchi, remembered hearing these words of wisdom when she was a child: "Never call out to others when you flee from a tsunami, because you will find yourselves standing around talking to each other. Just run away, and never, ever turn back."

Another Otsuchi resident, Yukari Kurosawa, was told a simpler adage when she was young: "If a big earthquake hits and the ocean draws back, run!"

Children practice *tendenko* during a tsunami drill held on Okinawa on the fifth anniversary of the tsunami.

Unfortunately, *tendenko* is easier to follow in theory than in reality. The Great Tohoku Earthquake struck during the workday, and after the shaking stopped, the first impulse of many residents, panicking because of the unusual strength of the earthquake, was to head for home. In Japan, many families live in multigenerational households, and people were concerned about elderly parents and grandparents. They rushed in the wrong direction.

Some were also confused by a glitch in the earthquake early warning system. Earthquake and tsunami warning systems have to act quickly, with limited data. In the first minutes after the fault ruptured, the Japan Meteorological Agency (JMA) estimated the magnitude of the quake at 7.9. Three minutes after the quake began, the agency issued a tsunami warning predicting waves up to 20 feet high in Miyagi prefecture and 10 feet in Iwate and Fukushima.

To residents of coastal towns in those regions, the height of the wave made all the difference. Seawalls protected most of the villages and towns on the Japanese coast. The walls varied in height depending on the town, but most were about 20 feet tall. They could easily deflect a 15-foot wave. A 25-foot wave might overflow the barriers, causing minor flooding and damage. But a 40-foot wave would easily overtop the walls and destroy everything in its path.

Minutes after the first warning, the tsunami swept past a GPS buoy, which measured its height. Based on those measurements, JMA issued a new warning about twenty-eight minutes after the earthquake. It predicted waves higher than 30 feet in Miyagi, and 20 feet in Iwate and Fukushima. For most, however, the revised warning arrived too late. The first waves reached the shore

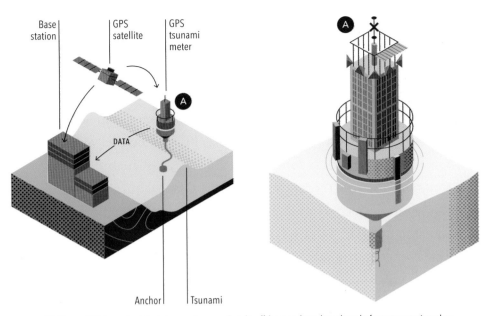

Base station | GPS satellite | GPS tsunami meter

DATA

Anchor | Tsunami

JAMA uses GPS buoys to detect changes in ocean height offshore and send an alarm before a tsunami reaches the shore. The buoys include GPS systems, transmitters, and solar panels. Satellites register changes in the buoys' position and transmit the data back to a base station, which issues alerts.

between fifteen and thirty minutes after the earthquake. They had already swept inland by the time the revised warning arrived.

In the town of Ishinomaki, dead center along the coast of Miyagi, residents were lulled into a false sense of security by the early tsunami predictions. After the earthquake, children and teachers at the Okawa Elementary School streamed out the doors wearing plastic safety helmets, standard equipment at any Japanese school. Nearby residents, who used the school as an evacuation center, joined them. Two and a half miles from the shore, they assumed they were safe. A few kids were picked up by worried parents. The rest—eighty students and twelve teachers—waited out the danger on the flat school grounds. Behind them was a 725-foot hill they could easily have climbed to safety.

Despite the confusion caused by the early tsunami predictions, hundreds of thousands of residents along the Tohoku coastline did flee. Buildings very close to the shore were clearly in danger. Evacuation sirens blared, and loudspeakers warned anyone within earshot to leave the area. And many wisely followed *tendenko*. But evacuation proved difficult. In the moments after the earthquake, smaller, secondary earthquakes, called aftershocks, continued to rattle the landscape. At the Otsuchi hospital, Yukari Kurosawa decided to walk home to check on her elderly mother. She didn't get far. "As I was crossing the bridge close to the hospital," she later remembered, "an aftershock hit and the bridge swayed wildly. If the bridge collapsed, I knew I'd die . . . so I turned back."

Those who tried to flee by car didn't fare much better. Roads were clogged with traffic. In some cases, they had crumbled.

Even as ordinary citizens fled to safety, emergency workers raced for the floodgates. Rivers and inlets from the sea provide an easy route for incoming waves, carrying tsunamis much farther inland than they could otherwise travel. Seawalls can't run across these inlets—the water needs to be able to flow back and forth under regular conditions. The solution is to build a dyke with floodgates—sliding panels that can be closed to seal off the opening—across the mouth of the river. The job of closing those massive gates fell to fire brigades.

Nestled between two mountains, the village of Fudai was a sitting duck for an incoming wave. The hills on either side of a cove would direct the water right down the middle, funneling it toward the village. But a 51-foot floodgate and an equally high seawall spanned the gap between the hills. After the earthquake struck, firefighters activated electric panels in the floodgate remotely, and most slid shut. But smaller side panels, probably damaged by the earthquake, wouldn't close. Four firefighters rushed to the jammed floodgate and struggled to fire up a backup generator. As they worked, the seawall blocked their view of the ocean, so they couldn't see what was coming. But they could hear it.

Before a tsunami arrives, the sea grows still. The water draws away from the shore, toward the approaching wave. People who have spent their entire lives surrounded by the constant rhythmic noise of the sea are suddenly met with silence.

And then the tsunami barrels in.

Survivors describe the sound of a tsunami as everything from a deafening rumble to a rasping hiss. The wave itself roars like a jet engine. As it moves, it picks up everything in its path.

The seawall at Fudai is 51 feet tall. Floodgates (blue) can be opened and closed to control the flow of water beneath the wall.

Giant ships, entire buildings, trucks, trees, and power poles snap, crunch, and grind.

In Fudai, the firefighters heard the growing thunder of an approaching wave as the stubborn panels slowly ground closed. They sped for safety as the monster wave poured over the seawall behind them.

—ᝰ—

For fifty-three-year-old Toshikazu Abe, the tsunami announced itself with an explosion. He had rushed home after the earthquake to check on his mother. Outside, loudspeakers were blaring an evacuation warning. Abe heard the warnings, but he didn't really believe the water could reach his home. Then he heard an explosion outside. "I heard a loud sound—*bam!*—like a telephone pole falling to the ground. I went out onto the balcony and saw a mountain of rubble surging right in front of me—parts of buildings, boats,

A wave of the tsunami pours over a seawall meant to protect the city of Miyako, about 150 miles north of Sendai, on March 11, 2011.

household objects. I stood there in stunned silence. The next moment, I was swept away by a giant wall of water and debris."

A woman named Katsuko Takahashi was trying to escape by car when the tsunami caught up to her. "I heard a rasping sound. Even inside the car, you could hear it. We were wondering what it was when, looking through the front windshield, all you could see were houses—houses everywhere."

One witness described the incoming wave as a "wall of pitch-black water." The tsunami coming ashore mixed with soil, sewage, oil, and rubble to form a fast-moving black sludge. It climbed higher and farther than anyone had thought possible, reaching a peak of more than 65 feet and as far as 3 miles inland.

In Ishinomaki, where students, teachers, and townspeople were still waiting on the school grounds, the wave surged up the Kitakami River and swallowed the Okawa Elementary School whole.

In the town of Kesennuma, the water first appeared innocuous enough, traveling far inland along the Okawa River. In advance of the tsunami, much of the water retreated. Then it began to flow back in. Like a layer of new water being poured over the old, it rolled forward. Curious spectators gathered along the concrete walls that lined the banks. They watched as small boats left on the river's banks were swept up and splintered by the power of the water. Still, it seemed unlikely that the river would overflow the high barriers designed to keep it from flooding. But the water kept coming. In minutes it had breached the walls and moved into the town with deadly speed. Residents climbed to the tops of high buildings and looked on in shock as a mass of inky water, littered with bits of buildings, ships, and Styrofoam cubes from a local factory, swept away their homes and neighbors. The water rose over the first and second stories of buildings before it stopped. That was the first wave. The second and third waves—the next rings in that ripple of displacement—followed close behind.

—⌒—

In Fukushima prefecture, the first tsunami wave reached the Daiichi nuclear plant at 3:27 P.M., forty minutes after the earthquake. It wasn't tall enough to reach the reactors. But the second wave easily overtopped a flood barrier and swamped all six. The backup generators that had kicked in after the earthquake sputtered out.

In Otsuchi, Ryoichi Usuzawa had found Taro and escaped the first wave by climbing onto his roof, carrying the dog. "From there," he remembered, "I could see the whole scene. Otsuchi was a giant washing machine . . . Cars and houses that had been swept away came smashing into my house with a grinding sound. The volume was incredible. Amid the noise, I heard voices saying, 'Please help—!' and hissing sounds from leaking propane tanks. Car horns were beeping from alarms that had short-circuited."

For people swept up by the water, survival was unlikely. As the flood sluiced inland, the current was fast and strong enough to drown even the most accomplished swimmer. That speed, coupled with the possibility of being crushed by massive amounts of debris—including entire houses—made the flood virtually impossible to escape.

As the tsunami swept through his home, Toshikazu Abe caught one last glimpse of his family. "I saw the exact moment when my mother was swept away by the wave. She was sitting on her chair," he remembered. Then he, too, was carried away. He was pinned by the rubble, but by a stroke of luck, his head was above water. "Thirty seconds passed by. I knew if I swallowed water I'd be done for. I was able to keep my head up, floating out of the water, but I was stuck in the rubble and couldn't move a muscle." When the first wave pulled back, the debris around him loosened and sank, and he was able to climb onto a nearby roof. "My body hurt so much that I couldn't move anymore . . . I eventually realized that I was bleeding everywhere."

At the hospital, patients were being moved to higher floors. Yukari Kurosawa followed them up. "Halfway up the stairs, I saw [that] the river already seemed about to burst its banks . . . An old man shouted, 'The water's rising! Everyone, everyone!' Hearing him shout, I reached the third floor and took two or three steps when, from

A photojournalist for a local newspaper in the town of Kamaishi is caught by the wave around 3:25 on March 11. Although the water rose to his chest and swept him about 100 feet, he managed to escape by grabbing on to a rope and climbing onto a 30-foot pile of coal.

below, there was a crunching, snapping sound. Turning to look behind me, [I saw that] a cloud of dust was rising from the stairs I had just climbed. If I had been only a little bit slower, I might have been swallowed up, too."

It was a cold day even for March, with temperatures barely reaching 40 degrees Fahrenheit (°F). And the water was freezing cold. Many of those who had managed to escape the flood were drenched and shivering, which made the fires that came next almost welcome.

Fires broke out when gas tanks and broken fuel lines ignited. Flames spread through the floating rubble and across the oily surface of the water. As they approached Toshikazu Abe, who was freezing on the roof, he had a strange thought. "This may sound crazy to you, and there was no doubt that I was in danger, but I thought to myself that the fire would be kind of warm and cozy. I wanted to warm myself up so I would be able to move and run away quickly."

After the first wave, Ryoichi Usuzawa clambered over the rubble between his rooftop and another building, holding on to a downed power line to keep from being swept away by the water. He clutched Taro the entire time. "At times, Taro's leash and collar would come loose, and time after time I contemplated how much easier it would be if I left him behind," he later said, "but when I saw his whimpering face . . . I was determined to save him." By the time the second wave came, he had managed to get inside the second floor of the building. He was relieved when the second wave ebbed. But not for long: "Just as the water went down around my ankles, then five or six propane tanks at the convenience store next door simultaneously exploded. It was scorching hot, I couldn't stand it. Sparks of fire were swarming around my feet. It was so hot, I thought my glasses might melt."

All along the coast of Iwate, Miyagi, and Fukushima, those who were lucky enough to escape the floodwaters scrambled to high ground. Some went to evacuation centers, only to find that the centers were in the path of the tsunami. Others who had found shelter had to evacuate again as fires spread.

Survivors gathered on hillsides and the roofs of tall buildings. From those safe perches, many watched the incoming waves in shock. "Honestly, I couldn't believe that only a minute ago this had been my hometown," remembers Toshikazu Abe. "But I also felt that I'd been saved; I had survived."

At sundown, it began to snow in earnest. Shivering people, many of them without blankets, food, or drinkable water, searched for dry clothes and huddled together for warmth. Many did not

Across the island of Honshu, people were stranded by the earthquake and tsunami. This woman and child spent the night in a shelter in Tokyo.

know what had happened to their families and friends. The lucky ones had been able to reach their loved ones by cell phone before the tsunami struck. Others wandered through evacuation centers, schools, and hospitals, looking for anyone with news.

Ryoichi Usuzawa and Taro had been rescued from the rooftop of a floating house by firefighters, who took them to an evacuation center at a local community hall. "It was very, very cold," he remembered later. "Within thirty minutes two elderly people passed away right in front of us. I thought, *Ah, I might die, too.* A public health nurse brought me some newspaper and when I wrapped myself with that, it was so warm. *How can a little bit of newspaper be so warm?* I wondered."

Sometime during the night, the snow stopped. The entire coastline was without power—no heat, no hot water, and no electric lights. In some towns, the sky glowed from the many fires sparked by the tsunami. But away from the light of the fires, many remembered seeing a spectacular blanket of stars.

In all, 154 square miles had been swallowed by waves and 127,000 homes destroyed. The survivors gathered at the Otsuchi hospital were trapped by the flood. But the hospital had blankets and fresh water, so they were better off than most. When the sun rose the next morning, a group of people gathered at a window that looked out over what was left of their town. As they stood, staring in shock, someone said, "We're all disaster victims now, aren't we?"

station blackout

Friday, March 11, 2011

Reactor Status

    Reactor 1: Scrammed
    Reactor 2: Scrammed
    Reactor 3: Scrammed
    Reactor 4: Shut down
    Reactor 5: Shut down
    Reactor 6: Shut down

While Ryoichi Usuzawa and Toshikazu Abe were fighting for survival in the tsunami waters and Yukari Kurosawa was trapped on the top floor of the Otsuchi hospital, workers at the Fukushima Daiichi power plant were at the beginning of what would be a long struggle to prevent another disaster from happening. About 200 miles from Otsuchi, the nuclear plant's operators spent the night of the tsunami working frantically in pitch-black control rooms desperately trying to stop a chain reaction that was spinning out of control.

A sprawling collection of reactors and support buildings, the Fukushima Daiichi plant covered almost 1.5 square miles along the coast of the Pacific Ocean. Its six nuclear reactors were lined up along the shore behind three long, low buildings that housed turbines. Four of the six reactors, numbers 1 through 4, fell within the town of Okuma to the south. Reactors 5 and 6 were part of the town of Futaba, about 500 feet to the north.

When most people hear the words "nuclear power plant," they picture a giant funnel tapering upward from a wide base and belching steam from the top. That's the shape of the nuclear plant where Homer Simpson works, and it's a common shape for nuclear plant cooling towers. But nuclear plants come in all shapes and sizes. At the Daiichi plant, the reactors were housed in six square buildings that had been painted a cheerful baby blue. A splattering of white on one corner of each building

This aerial view of the Fukushima Daiichi plant, taken shortly after the earthquake, shows the reactor buildings for units 1, 2, 3, and 4 (light blue). Turbine buildings lie between the reactors and the waterfront. The tall, scaffolded structures are exhaust chimneys.

mimicked the dappling of sun on the water. Inside was a series of containers, resting one inside the other like nesting dolls. At the heart of each nest, in the innermost container, was a nuclear boiling water reactor.

—∿—

At the most basic level, the majority of power plants work the same way: They boil water to create steam. The steam is used to turn a turbine, which generates electricity.

Nuclear power plants also use this process—they boil water to create steam that turns turbines. But while other power plants burn oil, gas, or coal to generate the heat that starts the process, nuclear power plants use uranium. And rather than burn it to

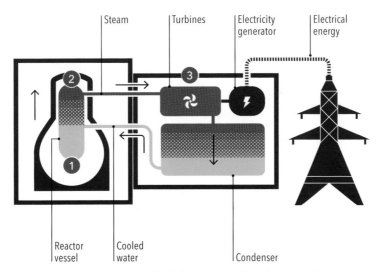

A turbine power plant takes the energy stored in fuel and converts it into a form that can be used to power buildings.
1. Fuel is converted into heat.
2. Water absorbs the heat and produces steam.
3. The steam travels through pipes and is blasted at a series of turbines, which rotate like pinwheels in the wind, powering the electric generator.

release energy, they use nuclear fission, a process that unlocks the energy stored inside a tiny, tiny package: the nucleus of an atom.

Everything on Earth, from your breakfast cereal, to your dog, to your cell phone, is made of some combination of elements. Break those elements down to their smallest parts, and you will find a series of atoms. At the center of each of those atoms lies the nucleus, a mash-up of even smaller particles called protons and neutrons. The number of protons in the nucleus determines which element the atom is, which is important for your cereal and your dog and your cell phone, but it's the neutrons that drive a nuclear chain reaction.

In nuclear fission, the goal is to split the nucleus of an atom in two. Most nuclear reactors use uranium 235 as fuel. For an atom, uranium 235 has a pretty enormous nucleus, packed with 92 protons and 143 neutrons. Its large size makes the nucleus of uranium 235 unstable—to break it apart, all nuclear operators need to do is add some loose neutrons to the mix.

Uranium 235 atom

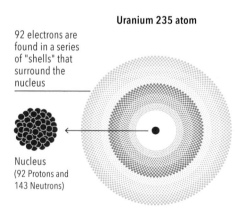

92 electrons are found in a series of "shells" that surround the nucleus

Nucleus
(92 Protons and 143 Neutrons)

Most of the physical size of an atom is made up of an electron cloud, which hovers around the nucleus.

When a neutron traveling at just the right speed strikes the nucleus of a uranium 235 atom, it is absorbed and the atom becomes even more unstable. That causes it to fission, breaking apart into two smaller atoms. But if you could somehow put the two pieces back together, you would discover that your taped-together atom weighed less than it did originally. The missing mass has been converted into energy.

Granted, it's not *a lot* of energy. Splitting one uranium atom releases about 200 million electron volts. That's about enough to make a single particle of dust jump—far from what's needed to turn the turbines of a power plant.

Fortunately, splitting a uranium atom doesn't just produce energy. When the atom splits, it also sends loose neutrons careening from the break. On average, two neutrons break away from each uranium atom that splits. And those neutrons just might hit two

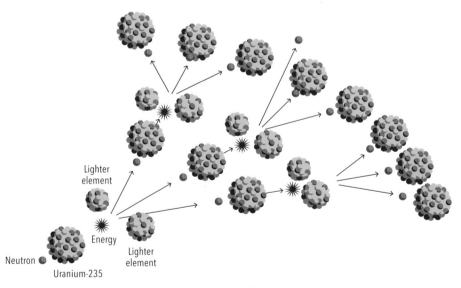

One fission can quickly become hundreds as neutrons spin off from each split and hit more nuclei.

more atoms, causing those to split. Those two atoms will each shed two neutrons, leaving four neutrons free to hit four atoms, which will release eight neutrons. On and on, the series of neutrons and atoms grows in what's known as a chain reaction. One fission becomes two, then four, eight, sixteen, and thirty-two. In a fully functioning nuclear reactor, trillions of atoms are fissioning at any point in time.

It all sounds easy enough, but in practice, starting that chain reaction is an extremely tricky process. When neutrons break free during fission, it's impossible to predict where they will go. They may be launched outward, into the shell of the nuclear reactor. Or they may head into the heart of the fuel but still fail to cause other atoms to fission. While uranium 235 fissions easily, nuclear fuel is not pure—it is made mostly of uranium 238, which does not fission. Reactors like the ones at Fukushima Daiichi increase the likelihood that those pinging neutrons will hit another uranium 235 nucleus by slowing them down.

The fuel used in a reactor is manufactured in pellets, which are stacked into rods and held together by a thin metal shell. In the reactor, each rod is surrounded by water. Water is made up of hydrogen and oxygen. And hydrogen atoms, as it turns out, are excellent at slowing down speeding neutrons. With just a single proton, the hydrogen nucleus has no particles that can be broken apart. When a speeding neutron hits a hydrogen nucleus, the hydrogen atom jumps, absorbing some of the neutron's momentum, but it does not break. When neutrons fly away from one fuel rod, the surrounding water slows them to the optimal speed before they reach the next uranium nuclei, making them more likely to

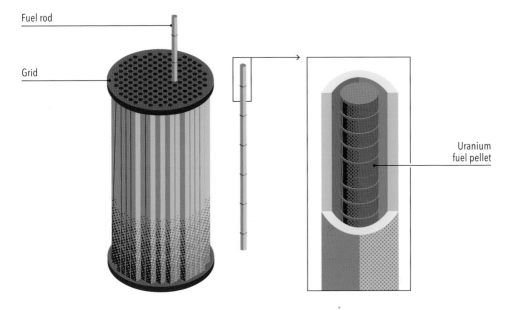

Fuel rods are rigged together in an assembly that allows neutrons to travel from one fuel rod to another.

create fission. When they do, energy from the atoms is released as heat.

Water is the workhorse of a boiling water reactor, performing three vital functions: It slows down the freed neutrons so the chain reaction is more likely to occur, but it also drives the turbines and cools the reactor. Water absorbs the heat generated by fission and evaporates into steam. That steam carries away the heat, and turns the turbine to generate electricity.

Generating electricity is the whole purpose of the reactor, but cooling it is equally important. Without the water to cool it, the reactor would quickly grow so hot that it would melt.

The challenge of running a nuclear reactor lies in keeping the number of bouncing neutrons inside it steady. When a uranium nucleus splits, its loose neutrons may never hit another uranium

235 nucleus. Or they may hit as many as three. That uncertainty means that nuclear engineers watch the overall reaction closely to make sure that things don't get out of hand. A reactor that is producing fewer neutrons than it is losing will eventually wind down, the chain reaction broken. In a reactor that produces more neutrons than it loses, the chain reaction will continue to grow, quickly spiraling out of control.

A reactor that is in balance, creating roughly the same number of neutrons as it is losing, is called critical. To keep things in that perfect zone, engineers insert control rods into the reactor. Held together by a long metal frame, the control rods are long, thin poles made of a material, often containing cadmium, that absorbs neutrons. They can be moved into the spaces between the fuel rods, where they soak up the neutrons bouncing between them and slow down the reaction. When the control rods are pulled out of the reactor core, the reaction speeds up. If they are inserted all the way in, neutrons can't travel between the fuel rods and the reactor grinds to a halt.

—᧬—

Before the quake, three of the reactors at Fukushima Daiichi, numbers 1, 2, and 3, had been critical, generating a little more than 2,000 megawatts, or approximately 2 billion watts, of electricity—enough to power about 400,000 homes. Reactors 4, 5, and 6 had been shut down for maintenance and inspection.

When the earthquake struck, it shook Daiichi with far more force than the plant was designed to withstand. That day, there were about 6,400 workers in the massive complex. They grabbed hard hats and scrambled under desks to wait it out. In the main office building, ceiling panels rained down, trapping workers under their desks. Lights crashed from the ceiling. Somewhere in the shaking, an electrical tower toppled. Buildings went black.

The plant had lost power, but it had multiple backups. Each reactor had two diesel generators, as well as batteries, that could power it in an emergency. The backup generators automatically kicked in.

The six reactors on the site were grouped in twos, with a control room between each pair. At the time of the earthquake, ninety-seven operators were in the three control rooms. In the control room for reactors 1 and 2, even as the room pitched and swayed, the operators moved quickly to monitor an emergency

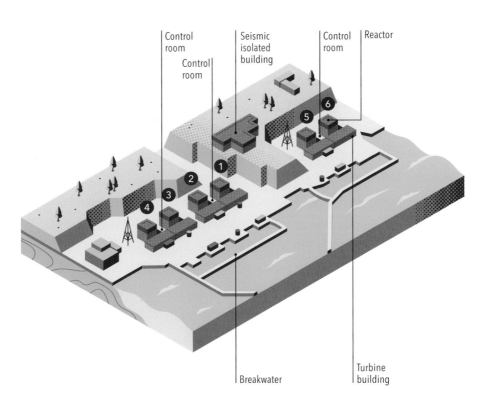

Control
room

Control
room

Seismic
isolated
building

Control
room

Reactor

Breakwater

Turbine
building

procedure known as a scram. Triggered by emergency systems, control rods automatically shot up into the reactor cores, putting a damper on the movement of neutrons between the fuel rods. Operators checked the backup cooling systems to make sure they were working properly. In the control room for reactors 3 and 4, operators couldn't check the backup systems until the quake had passed. In the end, though, the control rods were in and the chain reactions had been paused. It was a vanilla scram, with nothing remarkable to report. But everyone knew that a tsunami would be coming. The plant was located just feet from the ocean, and that meant workers needed to move to high ground. Outside the control rooms, they scrambled to evacuate. About two hundred people who were on the ocean side of the plant made a dash for the gates.

Nuclear power plants are some of the most closely guarded places in the world. In order to get to the plant exits on the other side of the complex, the ocean-side workers needed to go back into the main part of the plant through an entry gate. That meant a security check with metal detectors. The guards at the entry gate kept the workers waiting. One worker recalled the panic building among those trapped outside the gate. "Let us out of here! A tsunami may be coming!" they yelled. They worried that if they tried to climb the fence to flee, they could be prosecuted. Eventually, the guards allowed them to pass through.

Inside the complex, fallen office equipment had trapped some workers under desks and they needed to be freed by their co-workers. In the building housing reactor 3, a crane operator was stuck in the cockpit of his crane. His colleagues rushed in with a flashlight to help him find his way down.

On the inland side of the plant, workers gathered at the exit gates. Another worker, who asked to be called Kai Watanabe when he later told his story, remembers people standing in an orderly line to turn in their dosimeters—instruments that measure radiation exposure—and waiting as their supervisors counted the workers to make sure no one was missing. Once they'd made it through the gates, some, including Kai, rushed off to try to reach family members in Okuma and Futaba before the tsunami did.

Hundreds of employees who had been designated as emergency workers headed for an earthquake-proof structure called the seismic isolated building, which was set back from the water. To get in, they had to navigate more than 60 feet of stairs that had been covered in slippery sludge. "When I arrived," one worker remembered, "a ruptured ground pipe was spraying water like a geyser and had caused a mudslide that covered the stairs."

On the second floor, in the emergency response center, the plant superintendent, Masao Yoshida, was trying to get a handle on the situation. When the first two tsunami warnings, predicting 10- and 20-foot waves, were announced on TV, he ordered all workers to evacuate to either the seismic isolated building or high ground. The third tsunami warning, predicting a 32-foot wave, arrived too late.

At 3:27 P.M., just forty-one minutes after the earthquake, the first wave crashed into the Fukushima shore. Reactors 1 through 4 sat 33 feet above sea level; reactors 5 and 6 were at 42 feet above. All were safe from the first wave, which was only 18 feet high. But when the second wave barreled in ten minutes later, it was closer to 50 feet tall—about as high as a five-story building.

It easily rolled over the plant's 30-foot seawall, sweeping a tractor trailer into the building complex and pulling a massive oil tank into the ocean when it receded. Water swamped the turbine buildings on the ocean side of the reactors, and climbed 18 feet—about two stories—up the outsides of units 1 through 4.

A maintenance worker was in the reactor building at unit 2 when he heard rumbling in the basement. He raced for the stairs as seawater poured through a service entrance. He was soaking wet when he reached the control room on the top floor. Another worker, trying to reach a building near unit 4, was trapped at a security gate. He was trying to contact the guards using an intercom when the tsunami flooded in. "Just as I thought I was going to die with water encroaching from below," he later remembered, "a senior employee in the same situation broke the glass of the gate and escaped, and then helped me out by breaking the glass on my side. When I did escape from the confinement, water had inundated to the height of immediately below my jaw. I was really scared."

A car is tossed like a tub toy by a wave that inundated the North side of the Fukushima Daiichi plant. This photo was taken from the fourth floor of the plant's radiation waste treatment facility.

Despite the close call, he was fortunate. Two of his co-workers, who had been sent to the basement of unit 4 to check the status of the reactor, drowned.

—ᴧ—

Sheltered behind the reactors in the windowless control rooms, the operators couldn't see or hear the incoming waves. But they knew they were in trouble. In the minutes after the scram, warning lights had lit up and alarms had started blaring. At 3:36, the lights on the control panels in the unit 1 and 2 control room began to flicker. Then they snapped off. The operators were plunged into darkness on one side of the room. On the other, dim emergency lighting cast a glow over the stunned crew. An eerie silence settled.

A nuclear reactor control room looks like something out of a classic Cold War movie. Most reactors were built long before

The unit 3 control room at Fukushima Daiichi in September of 2010, about six months before the tsunami.

fast, compact computers were available, and Fukushima Daiichi, which was commissioned in the 1970s, was no exception. They are complicated contraptions with hundreds of parts, every one of which feeds back through wires to the control room. Gauges and switches that crowd the control room walls constantly report on the state of the reactor. From there, the team of operators can track every tiny detail of the reactor's function. On a usual day, operators are making sure that the chain reaction clips along at just the right rate for power production. On March 11, they needed those instruments to prevent a meltdown.

—〰—

The three active reactors at the plant had successfully scrammed. But operators knew that the scram is only the first step in reaching what is known as cold shutdown.

When a uranium atom fissions, the two pieces that are left are radioactive. The broken nuclei hold too many neutrons for the new atoms—that's why neutrons break loose. But they don't necessarily fly off immediately. The atoms shed them over time. So, even after the control rods have been inserted into the reactor core and the chain reaction has been stopped, atoms in the fuel rods that have already split continue to release energy, creating what is known as decay heat. It can take up to twenty-four hours for a properly functioning nuclear reactor to reach cold shutdown—the point at which the temperature of the core dips below boiling.

Until then, cooling systems need to run or the water in the reactor will quickly boil off, leaving the fuel exposed. Without water to keep the fuel rods cool, temperatures in the core can climb as high as 5,100°F—hotter than a lava flow. Hot enough to melt the fuel rods and allow them to sink right through the bottom of the reactor.

All three of the scrammed reactors had emergency cooling systems. Units 2 and 3 each had a reactor core isolation cooling system, or RCIC (pronounced "Ricksy"). The RCIC system pumps water from storage tanks called suppression pools into the reactor. The pumps are powered by turbines, which are driven by steam coming from the reactor. But unit 1, the oldest reactor in the plant, had an outdated cooling system known as an isolation condenser.

The isolation condenser is what's known as a passive system— it doesn't require outside power. All it needs is for two valves to be opened: one at the top, to allow steam from the core into the system, and one at the bottom, to allow cooled water to drip back into the core.

In the minutes following the earthquake, operators had opened the valves. The system was up and running.

—ᴧ—

Both the isolation condenser in unit 1 and the RCIC systems in units 2 and 3 should have continued to work without power. But they'd taken a severe beating from a major earthquake. And in the minutes before they were flooded, the RCIC systems had automatically shut down because there was too much water in the reactors. The batteries that supplied power to the instrument panels in unit 3 were still running. But when the second wave swept through, the operators in the control room for units 1 and 2 lost all power. They had no way to tell what was going on. For people who spent their workdays watching the ups and downs of reactor pressure and heat, and making constant adjustments to keep things running safely, it was a worst-case scenario.

In the emergency response center, Superintendent Yoshida knew they were in serious trouble. He immediately notified the company's headquarters in Tokyo that two of Daiichi's reactors, 1 and 2, had likely lost their cooling. But Tokyo was 190 miles away. Between the plant and any outside help lay a region that had just been devastated by a massive flood. The reality was that the employees at Fukushima Daiichi were on their own.

To make matters worse, phone lines that should have allowed the emergency response team to communicate with the operators in the control rooms were down. The only way to communicate was in person, so workers had to carry messages back and forth between the emergency response center and the control rooms. Along their route, manhole covers had been blown off by the force of the waves, turning the roads between buildings into an obstacle course of open holes lurking beneath the standing water. What's more, hundreds of aftershocks continued to rattle Fukushima, threatening to shake broken pieces loose from buildings at any time. And in the hours following the second wave, five more washed into the site. Workers could never be sure when the next wave would come, making the short trip potentially deadly.

Yoshida and his team started brainstorming. They didn't have a lot to work with. Much of the heavy equipment outside the reactors had been swept away by the waves. A tractor trailer had been pushed across an access door to unit 4. A storage tank blocked the road leading to units 1 through 4. Everything on the bottom floor of the reactor buildings—including the diesel generators they so desperately needed to run the reactors—had been submerged in salt water. And despite hundreds of hours of emergency training, no one really knew what to do next. Using flashlights in the dark, windowless room, they combed through operating manuals. But the possibility of a nuclear reactor losing every source of power at once had never seemed real, so no one had thought through solutions ahead of time.

A photo taken a little over an hour after the tsunami struck Fukushima Daiichi shows the damage outside the unit 1 building.

A team of nuclear engineers and high-level Tokyo Electric Power Company (TEPCO) staff had gathered around a horseshoe of tables laden with computers in the emergency response center. Sitting at the head table and barking orders to the hundreds of workers who had crammed into the space after the quake, Superintendent Yoshida began to take stock of his reactors. It was an enormous task, made much worse by the fact that each of the six reactors had risk factors that could cause unique problems. While units 4, 5, and

6 were shut down before the earthquake and tsunami, those three re-actors still held spent fuel in storage pools, and even spent fuel needs to be kept cool. Fortunately, a backup generator in unit 6 had been installed beyond the reach of the flood. They could run a line to that generator to keep unit 5 running, too. Because unit 3 still had battery power, operators were able to restart its RCIC system and knew that water was flowing into the reactor. But units 1 and 2, they feared, could be in danger. They desperately needed to get a better sense of what was happening inside those reactors.

They had a brief glimpse at 4:42 P.M., about an hour after the power went out. Operators managed to get a reading off a water-level indicator inside the reactor in unit 1. Measuring how much water had been lost since the tsunami, they did some calculations and realized that they had less than two hours before the water level in the reactor dropped below the tops of the fuel rods. Once that happened, the rods would begin to melt.

At 5:19, operators went back to unit 1 to try to get another reading off the water meter. When they opened the double door to the building, the Geiger–Müller counter they were carrying to measure radiation maxed out and they had to abandon their task.

In the meantime, workers had been searching for a power source for the control panels. They fanned out across the plant, searching cars and trucks for batteries that hadn't been damaged by the flood.

It was a little past 6:00 P.M. before they managed to hook up enough batteries to get the first gauges working. Then they made an unwelcome discovery: the two valves that needed to be open to allow cooled water to flow from the isolation condenser back into the reactor of unit 1 were closed. When the power cut out, the system had misread the signal as a steam leak.

The condenser was not working. They needed to come up with a plan to get cooling water into the reactor.

—ᴧ—

The reactor vessel, which holds the fuel, control rods, and coolant, lies at the center of a nuclear reactor building. It's shaped like a capsule and made of 8-inch-thick steel. The reactor is surrounded by a containment structure, a chamber of steel-reinforced concrete as much as 5 feet thick—strong enough to hold the contents of the reactor if the steel vessel fails. Surrounding that is the giant steel building that we see from the outside, known as secondary containment. In an emergency, the containment should trap gases that might escape from the inner chambers, but we rely on the reactor

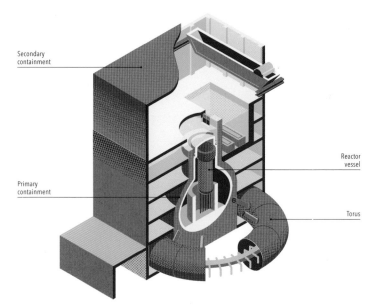

The steel reactor vessel at the heart of each reactor building is surrounded by a thick concrete containment vessel, designed to hold radioactive materials that might escape from the reactor in an emergency.

vessel to keep a nuclear reaction—and the radiation it produces—contained. Like a pressure cooker, it is designed to hold together even as extreme amounts of steam build up inside it.

Think of it this way: When you boil a pot of water, water molecules in the form of steam escape from the pot and drift into your kitchen. If you put a lid over the pot, though, the steam collects underneath. As more and more steam fills the pot, the water molecules become more and more crowded. They bang into each other, and the pressure in the pot rises, causing the lid to dance.

Pressure cookers are designed with heavy locks that hold the lid on the pot, even when an enormous amount of steam has built up beneath it. A reactor vessel is the same. But with its 8-inch-thick walls, it can withstand far more pressure than your pot.

That's a problem if you're trying to get more water into the reactor vessel. The steam inside presses against the walls of the vessel with an enormous amount of force. The pressure of the water coming in has to be stronger, or it won't be able to push its way into the space.

Before workers could add water to reactor 1, they would have to vent the reactor, releasing steam to lower the pressure. That meant opening the closed valves, and for that, they needed power. The control room sent a message to the emergency response center requesting more batteries so they could open the safety valves and vent the extra steam.

But in the chaos of the emergency response center, the request didn't seem urgent. The emergency response team, frantically running down scenarios on all six reactors, hadn't gotten the news that the cooling system in unit 1 was down. Workers had reported that they heard hissing sounds from the reactor, and steam was puffing from a vent on the side of the building—both of which seemed to indicate that the isolation condenser was working. The emergency response team believed unit 2 was in greater danger, and the team members had focused their attention there. The control room operators, powerless in the dark, were left waiting.

—⌁—

By about 9:00 P.M., the water in unit 1 had boiled down to below the tops of the reactor's fuel rods, and they were most likely already melting. But no one knew the situation was that dire. At 9:19, operators used battery power to read the water level inside the reactor, and the gauge showed that the fuel rods were still covered by about 8 inches of water. It was a far cry from the 20 feet of water that would normally be found above the fuel rods, but it looked as though they were at least covered.

As it turned out, the water-level indicator was malfunctioning. By then, the melting fuel rods had probably already begun to pool at the bottom of the reactor in a molten mass called corium. It was only a matter of time before the molten corium would eat through the reactor vessel and fall to the floor of the concrete containment chamber.

—⌁—

In the pitch-black of the control rooms, some of the operators wondered what they were doing there. Most of them had families nearby. Some had managed to send messages before the tsunami,

Operators read instruments by flashlight in the units 1 and 2 control room on March 23, 2011.

but all contact was lost after the power went out. The stress of waiting helplessly wore on them. There were no working toilets, and very little food. A supervisor remembers some of his workers begging to go home. "We were thrown into confusion over the question *Is it worth us staying here helplessly . . . ? Why are we staying here?* I pleaded with them to stay."

The question grew more pressing around 10:00 P.M., when radiation levels in unit 1 began to climb. Workers were ordered to stay out of the reactor building. Rising radiation could mean only one thing: that radioactive isotopes had somehow gotten out of the reactor vessel.

Although they did not know it then, the steel reactor vessel had been breached, and the radioactive fuel was oozing into the drywell, the open space in the primary containment chamber. Even worse, though, a chemical reaction that was occurring in the high heat of the reactor core was producing highly flammable hydrogen gas.

meltdown

Saturday, March 12, 2011

```
┌─ Reactor Status ──────────────────────────────┐
│     Reactor 1: Melted down                     │
│     Reactor 2: Scrammed                        │
│     Reactor 3: Scrammed                        │
│     Reactor 4: Shut down                       │
│     Reactor 5: Shut down                       │
│     Reactor 6: Shut down                       │
│                                                │
└────────────────────────────────────────────────┘
```

The hundreds of thousands of people who had fled their homes the day before awoke to a very different Japan on March 12. Friday morning had been full of routines for most: packing school lunches, eating a hasty breakfast before work, catching the bus. By Saturday, the routines of their previous lives had come to a sudden halt. There was no longer a school or a bus. There was no kitchen to make breakfast in. Saturday was a day to take stock.

More than 400,000 people were without homes. Many were stranded on rooftops and hills, surrounded by the water and wreckage left behind by the tsunami.

While the basic facts of the earthquake and tsunami were the same for everyone on the Tohoku coast, the details for each town were unique. The earthquake had caused much of the coast to sink, and water remained trapped in many towns, turning them into lakes. In others, the water had already retreated, leaving behind a thick jumble of mangled cars, destroyed boats, and crumbled buildings. Some towns were still burning as the sun rose—oil tanks and gas canisters broken open by the force of the water fueled the flames. In Ishinomaki, the Okawa Elementary School lay beneath a layer of thick, black mud that was several feet deep. It would be days before the families of the children who were lost there learned their fates.

Every survivor had a different story. Some, like Ryoichi Usuzawa, had lost their homes but still had their families. Usuzawa had found his wife the night before at the local evacuation center. Others had lost a child, or a parent, but still had the

Buildings were swept from their foundations and left in pieces up and down the coast of Tohoku. The rubble would remain for months–this photo was taken on March 25, 2011, two weeks after the tsunami.

rest of their family. Many had lost their entire families. Toshikazu Abe would never see his wife or mother again.

Usuzawa, who helped out as a greeter at the evacuation center, remembered the grim accounting that the survivors went through in the days following the wave: "Someone asks you, . . . 'How about your family, was everyone safe?' and you respond, 'Yes, we are all okay,' but then you ask them 'How about you?' and they say something like, 'We had a family of five but now we are three . . .' All I could do was hug them."

Help would not be coming anytime soon. Cell phone service was down, and landlines were nonexistent. In some cases, there wasn't anyone to call, anyway. Fire stations, police stations, and municipal centers had been carried away with everything else. The Tohoku region, dotted with tiny farming and fishing villages,

A woman searches among the mud and rubble in Otsuchi for her missing nephew five days after the tsunami.

is famous for its remoteness at the best of times. Now, with roads blocked and crumbled, it would take days for any help to come from the outside. So the survivors of the tsunami began the hard work of finding food, shelter, and missing loved ones on their own. They had no way of knowing about the disaster that was unfolding at the Fukushima Daiichi plant.

The uranium pellets that form nuclear fuel rods are held together by a thin coating, called cladding, of the metal zirconium. Under normal conditions, the zirconium does its job well, reinforcing the sturdy rods without getting in the way of zinging neutrons. But zirconium has one drawback: At extremely high heat, it reacts with steam. That reaction produces potentially explosive hydrogen gas—lots of it—and Fukushima Daiichi had passed that temperature threshold hours before. Hydrogen gas was building up in reactor 1, and the increasing volume of the gas, combined with the steam created by decay, was making the pressure in the containment vessel climb. By 11:00 P.M. the night before, the pressure had already exceeded the maximum that the vessel was meant to hold. That posed a serious problem for getting water into the reactor, and it was also dangerous in its own right. If the pressure got high enough, the vessel could break open, sending radiation into the air around the reactor. Operators needed to get water into the reactor to slow the runaway reactions. Their best bet for doing that was to vent steam through the torus.

The torus, or suppression pool, sits like a giant hollow doughnut below the reactor vessel. When pressure in the reactor gets too high, a safety valve opens and allows steam to escape into the torus, where it condenses back into water. Steam that passes through the torus is scrubbed of most of its radioactive isotopes before it leaves the building, a vast improvement over allowing the steam to enter the environment without any intervention.

But before operators could open the vents, which would likely still release some radioactive steam into the air, they needed approval from the government. And they needed to give residents of the nearby towns time to evacuate.

Operators also needed to find a way to open two valves without working controls. That would mean sending workers into the reactor building, where the radiation levels had been rising.

Supervisors planned to send teams in one at a time to make rescue easier in case they ran into problems. To reduce the danger of health effects that might appear later, they opted for older volunteers. Still, when Takeyuki Inagaki, a maintenance manager, asked for volunteers for the dangerous job, many young workers raised their hands. He was moved to tears. "To go into a pitch-black reactor building, with the containment pressure so high . . . ," he later remembered, "it felt like we were putting together a suicide squad."

It would be a grueling task, so they selected workers who they thought were strong enough to complete it successfully and divided them into teams of three. Then the teams began training for their mission, practicing to make sure they knew where they needed to go inside the darkened building. Superintendent Yoshida told his team they would need to be ready to vent by 9:00 A.M. But they weren't idle in the hours before then.

Overnight, other response teams had been formed to clean up debris so workers could get to the reactor buildings, and to set up vital systems to get power and water to them. One worker remembered seeing some of the members of those response teams in the emergency response center as they were getting ready to go out to the reactors. "I'll never forget the expressions on the faces of the employees assembled into those response teams," he later said. "Their faces, in the face of lethal danger, were white as a sheet . . . Every single one of them was trembling; they were truly scared."

A working generator to power the lights in the reactor 1 control room had finally been found, taking the operators out of the dark for the first time in hours. One of the teams had labored throughout the night to lay a high-voltage cable that could carry electricity to units 1 and 2 from an electrical truck. Starting around midnight, forty workers had begun laying 650 feet—about 3,000 pounds' worth—of the heavy cable. It was slow going. Hundreds of aftershocks rocked the plant overnight. When a particularly large one hit, the workers had to scurry back to safety for an hour to make sure that another tsunami wouldn't be following. At 4:00 A.M., radiation levels outside the unit 1 reactor had begun to rise, and the workers had to stop yet again.

At 5:44 A.M. on Saturday, the prime minister of Japan, Naoto Kan, issued the evacuation order for everyone within 6 miles of the plant—about 45,000 people altogether. For many of the refugees sheltering at evacuation centers, the order to evacuate was their first indication that something had gone seriously wrong at the nuclear plant, and it left them with a terrible choice.

A man named Noriyo Kimura had lived two miles from the plant. The tsunami had swept away his home, along with his wife, father, and a daughter. He desperately wanted to search for his missing family members. But he had one remaining daughter who had not been in the tsunami's path. He knew that, in order to protect his surviving daughter from the radiation the plant might release, he had to abandon the faint sliver of hope that one of those swept away could have survived.

Many faced the same stark decision: Staying would endanger their health and that of others who had escaped the tsunami. But evacuating meant abandoning their plans to search through the rubble for loved ones who might still be alive.

Residents in the towns of Futaba and Okuma, as well as nearby Namie and Tomioka, clambered onto buses bound for towns farther inland. Those who had working cars or places aboard buses were lucky. The governments of Okuma and Futaba found themselves overwhelmed. Jin Ishido, who was in charge of crisis management for the town of Okuma, remembers: "It was complete chaos. We were not prepared. We had no protection, no protective gear, no experts. Our communication lines were disrupted . . . We didn't have contingency plans for hospitals—even the firefighters didn't have a plan."

At the Futaba hospital, 209 patients and the hospital staff prepared to evacuate. Finding buses to move them out proved a monumental task. Katsutaka Idogawa, the mayor of Futaba, helped organize the patients who were being evacuated, directing them onto buses to move them out of the danger zone. But 130 patients who were confined to their beds, as well as 98 residents of a nursing home who could not be moved, were left behind without staff to care for them. The staff had been told that Japan Special Defense Forces would be there soon to move the bedridden patients. In reality, it would be two days before they arrived. In the meantime, the patients were left without heat, electricity, or basic care. Four had died by the time help arrived, and fourteen more died as they were being moved. Thirty-five more patients were left behind once again and wouldn't be rescued for two more days.

Frustrated that it was taking so long for venting to begin, Prime Minister Kan flew to the plant to meet with Yoshida at 7:00 A.M. But even with the leader of the country pushing them to move

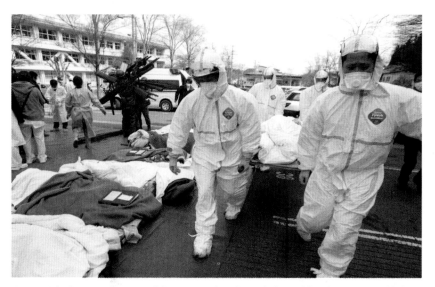

Events at Fukushima Daiichi prevented these patients from the Futaba hospital from being evacuated before Sunday, March 13.

forward, the operators had to wait. They had learned that the evacuation wasn't complete, and they did not want to vent while residents of any nearby town were still scrambling to leave.

At 9:04, the nine volunteers finally headed for the unit 1 reactor to begin venting. The first team, which went to the second floor, managed to open its valve. But the second, which aimed to open the valve on the torus, was pushed back by heat and radiation. As they entered the basement, the sound of the steam thundering into the suppression pool was overwhelming. The torus room, normally dry, was hazy with steam. The team's task was to open a valve that would allow steam to escape from the suppression pool through a pipe to the outside. To do that, they would need to walk out onto the surface of the torus.

One worker took a tentative step.

His shoes melted.

A team member's dosimeter indicated that he had already been exposed to the maximum amount of radiation he was allowed to receive in a year. They had no choice but to abandon their mission.

—⌇—

The operators had been on shift for thirty hours since the earthquake. They had been working constantly, trying to push their exhausted brains to develop creative solutions to one problem after another. Rest wasn't an option. They came up with a new plan to blow the valve open from a distance using an air compressor, and began to search for one in the jumbled mess of the nuclear plant. It was 2:00 P.M. before they finally found one and installed it. To the operator's relief, the pressure in the drywell finally began to fall at about 2:30. It looked like the vent was working, letting out steam and taking the pressure off the containment structure.

In reality, the pressure may have been going down for a far more ominous reason: At the top of the containment structure is a heavy steel lid that can be opened for reactor maintenance. It normally takes a crane to move the massive dome, which is held down by dozens of oversized bolts. But the prolonged high pressure in the chamber below it had worked the bolts loose, and hydrogen gas was escaping into the reactor building.

At 3:30 on Saturday afternoon, the forty-member electrical team finally finished connecting power to the unit 1 building. Six minutes later, all of their work would be undone.

At 3:36, somewhere in the unit 1 building, a spark met the cloud of hydrogen gas. In an instant, the molecules surrounding the

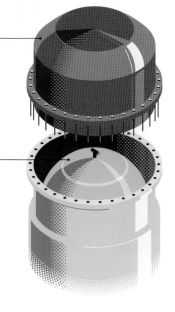

Steel
containment
vessel lid

Reactor
vessel

spark burst into flame. In just a few milliseconds more, the heat had raced through all of the gas in the building, setting it alight. Superheated air leaped outward in a thundering explosion, shredding the walls of

Encircled by hefty bolts, the primary containment vessel lid can be removed for maintenance. The many bolts were worked loose by the pressure of the hydrogen gas building up below the lid.

the reactor building and sending a cloud of white smoke and debris billowing into the air. Workers, in the middle of injecting water and restoring power, were rocked by the blast. "[The] windows of the fire truck were shattered," remembers one of them. "Things looked distorted to me for a moment. Then I felt as if I was floating at the same time as [I heard] a tremendous roaring sound . . . I was showered with rubble from in front like a rocket." The control room shook and filled with a cloud of white dust. For the second time in twenty-four hours, the lights flickered out.

The "rubble" that rained down on the workers was probably pieces of the steel sheeting that had surrounded the reactor building. Debris from the explosion reached even farther afield, showering stragglers from the evacuation of Futaba. "I was in front of the hospital," Mayor Idogawa remembers, "telling people to evacuate. Putting people on buses and cars, just sending people out. That's when I heard the boom of the explosion. It must've been parts of the building and other debris that came

The unit 1 building after the explosion on March 12.

raining down. We're close by, so it was the heavier stuff that came down on us . . . And I thought, *Let's just leave this place. Just get the kids out* . . . I just wanted everyone out."

When the smoke cleared at the plant, the entire roof and top third of the reactor 1 building had been reduced to a smoking steel skeleton. Five workers had been injured.

DAY 3

evacuation

Sunday, March 13, 2011

```
┌─ Reactor Status ──────────────────────────────────┐
│     Reactor 1: Melted down/building destroyed      │
│     Reactor 2: Scrammed                            │
│     Reactor 3: Scrammed                            │
│     Reactor 4: Shut down                           │
│     Reactor 5: Shut down                           │
│     Reactor 6: Shut down                           │
└────────────────────────────────────────────────────┘
```

You probably think of yourself as a single, solid object. But look closer. You are really a collection of parts: organs and bones, tendons and teeth. Zoom in even more, and you'll see cells and the molecules they are made from. Look even closer and you'll see that you are a universe of atoms.

At the atomic level, the lines that separate our bodies from our environment are not as definite as you might think. Hold my hand, and the atoms on the surface of your skin interact with the atoms on mine. If you're unlucky enough to do it on a cold, dry day, loose electrons might leap from my hand to yours, giving you a static electric shock.

Your atoms are tiny—so very, very small that it would take

about 100,000 of them, arranged in a line, to reach across the diameter of a single hair from your head. That tininess has advantages. Our individual atoms can't be damaged by large-scale events. Long after you die, your atoms will still be here as part of the soil, rock, water, and air—perhaps even another animal. And yet atoms can be affected by things on their own miniature scale, things so small that they are invisible to us.

It's our atoms that make us vulnerable to radiation.

Put simply, radiation is energy. It travels through our world as particles or waves, and it is everywhere. Solar radiation warms our planet and feeds the plants we need to survive. Radio waves, another form of radiation, carry information from your Wi-Fi router to your computer and from cell phones to the nearest cell tower. Visible light is also radiation.

—◊—

Each of our atoms holds protons and neutrons at its center in a super-dense mass called the nucleus. Electrons hover around

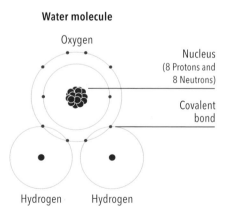

Water molecule

Oxygen

Nucleus
(8 Protons and
8 Neutrons)

Covalent
bond

Hydrogen   Hydrogen

When two or more atoms are bonded, as in water, they form a molecule.

the nucleus in a cloud. This tiny galaxy forms its own balance between the positive charge of the protons in its nucleus and the negative charge of the electrons that surround them. But if a radioactive particle or wave has enough energy, it can knock electrons out of an atom altogether, creating an ion. Once an electron flies the coop, the electrical charge of the atom changes. But here's the thing: It is the atom's electrical charge that determines how it behaves in relationship to the atoms around it. When an atom that is part of a molecule loses an electron, it lets go of the other atoms, breaking the molecule apart and destroying our tiniest building blocks.

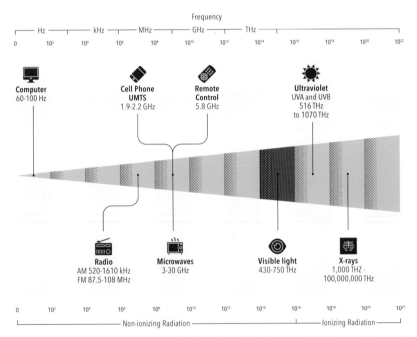

Radiation can be divided into different types based on the wavelengths it emits. Radiation on the low end of the spectrum (to the left on this chart) has long wavelengths and short frequencies. Only radiation of especially short lengths and high frequencies (on the right side of the chart), known as ionizing radiation, has enough energy to affect our health.

Most of the radiation that surrounds us lacks the energy to do us harm. If you arrange all of the types of radiation in the world on a chart according to the amount of energy they produce, it's only the radiation at the top end of the lineup, called ionizing radiation, that has enough power to do damage.

How dangerous is ionizing radiation? That depends entirely on how much of it you are exposed to. Radiation *can* alter atoms. But the human body has more than a few to spare—altogether, there are about 7 octillion atoms in the average adult. That's a 7 with 27 zeroes after it, or 7 billion billion *billion* atoms. While small doses of radiation may do some damage, they are unlikely to affect enough atoms to cause real trouble. But when the human body is exposed to massive doses of radiation, cells begin to die.

If they're released during a nuclear accident, the same neutrons that ping around inside the nuclear reactor breaking apart uranium atoms can careen through a worker's body. Radiation might knock out a piece of the cell's DNA, change the structure of the cell wall, or alter the thickness of the fluid in the cell. In the end, the effect is the same: a damaged cell cannot function properly. When enough cells are damaged, the body begins to break down.

The course of radiation sickness, also called acute radiation syndrome, varies widely depending on what kind of radiation was absorbed and where in the body it causes the most damage. But some effects are universal. In high enough doses, radiation sickness almost always causes nausea, headaches, and a general feeling of illness that can last anywhere from a few hours to two days. After that, the symptoms disappear for a time. With milder poisoning, this period of normalcy can last up to two weeks; in severe cases, it ends in as little as five days. Then the real impact of the radiation

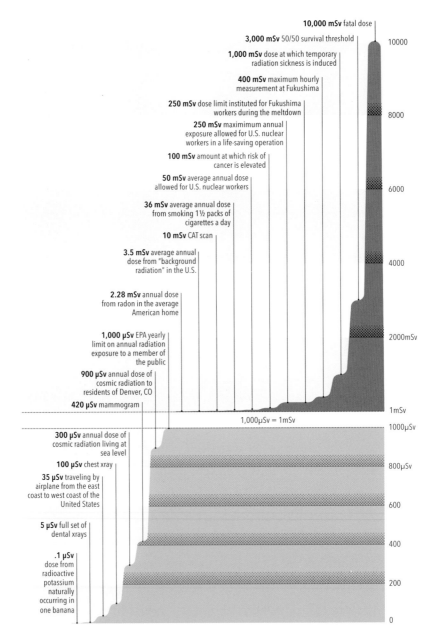

10,000 mSv fatal dose

3,000 mSv 50/50 survival threshold

1,000 mSv dose at which temporary radiation sickness is induced

400 mSv maximum hourly measurement at Fukushima

250 mSv dose limit instituted for Fukushima workers during the meltdown

250 mSv maximimum annual exposure allowed for U.S. nuclear workers in a life-saving operation

100 mSv amount at which risk of cancer is elevated

50 mSv average annual dose allowed for U.S. nuclear workers

36 mSv average annual dose from smoking 1½ packs of cigarettes a day

10 mSv CAT scan

3.5 mSv average annual dose from "background radiation" in the U.S.

2.28 mSv annual dose from radon in the average American home

1,000 µSv EPA yearly limit on annual radiation exposure to a member of the public

900 µSv annual dose of cosmic radiation to residents of Denver, CO

420 µSv mammogram

300 µSv annual dose of cosmic radiation living at sea level

100 µSv chest xray

35 µSv traveling by airplane from the east coast to west coast of the United States

5 µSv full set of dental xrays

.1 µSv dose from radioactive potassium naturally occurring in one banana

10000

8000

6000

4000

2000mSv

1mSv

$1,000µSv = 1mSv$

1000µSv

800µSv

600

400

200

0

Naturally occurring radiation can be found everywhere–even at low levels in many of the foods we eat regularly. It is only at higher levels of exposure that it poses a threat. The base unit in this chart is the sievert (Sv): "µSv" stands for "microsievert," which is one millionth of a sievert, and "mSv" stands for "millisievert," which is one thousandth of a sievert.

strikes, with grisly symptoms that range from hair loss and extreme fatigue to the destruction of bone marrow and internal bleeding.

The Japanese Nuclear Regulation Authority measures radiation exposure in sieverts, a unit of measure that takes into account the strength and type of radiation and indicates the likely impact a given amount of radiation will have on the human body. (In the United States, a similar unit of measure called a rem is often used.) A person exposed to 1 sievert (Sv) of radiation suffers light radiation poisoning and has a 90 percent chance of survival. Around 4 Sv, the odds of survival drop to 50 percent. At 10 Sv, exposure is always fatal.

It sounds terrifying, but the odds of the average person encountering that kind of radiation are minuscule. It can only be found in environments where nuclear fission is occurring—in nuclear weapons and nuclear power plants.

The heart of a nuclear reactor seethes with deadly radioactivity. In the 1950s and '60s, the U.S. Air Force ran a series of experiments in a secluded stretch of woods 50 miles from Atlanta, Georgia. The Georgia Nuclear Aircraft Laboratory ran a 10-million-watt nuclear reactor completely unshielded. Everything within 1,000 feet of the reactor died. And that really means *everything*, from trees and birds to single-celled organisms and viruses.

On a normal day at a nuclear plant, workers are completely shielded from the radiation inside the reactor by the vessel's thick steel casing, by the water that covers the fuel rods, and by the thick concrete of the containment chamber. The average worker's radiation exposure is measured in millisieverts (mSv)—thousandths of sieverts. In Japan, a law set the maximum exposure allowed for a nuclear power plant worker under normal conditions at 50 mSv a year, or 100 mSv over five years. Nuclear workers carry dosimeters, badges that keep track of how much radiation they have encountered over time.

Nuclear plant workers know that if they need to enter an area where they may be exposed to radiation, there are three factors that can reduce their exposure: time, distance, and shielding.

If you've ever had a dental X-ray, you've seen these principles in action. Before starting the X-ray machine, the dentist always leaves the room, putting distance between herself and the radiation source. That's because radiation spreads out as it travels, making it less likely to strike you the farther away you are.

Leaving the room also reduces the amount of time that the dentist is exposed to X-rays. The short burst pointed at your teeth is no problem for you, since that happens only once every year or so, but if dentists stood right next to every patient they took X-rays of, they'd be getting exposed—at close range—many times a day.

1

Time
Less time spent near source: less radiation received

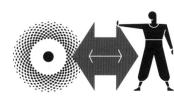

2

Distance
Greater distance from source: less radiation received

3

Shielding
Sheltering behind a shield: less radiation received

The same is true for nuclear power plant workers. Since the reactor is continually producing radiation, shortening their time near it reduces the amount of radiation workers are likely to absorb.

You probably also remember that the dentist placed a heavy lead bib over you before running the machine. The lead acted as a shield, blocking almost all of the X-rays from reaching your body.

For every type of radiation, there is some material that it is unable to travel through. In a nuclear power plant, water serves as a shield, slowing down and capturing neutrons, as do the steel walls of the reactor vessels and the thick concrete of the primary containment chamber. On a normal day, those shields prevent radiation from reaching workers and any other people nearby. But March 13, 2011, wasn't a normal day—the water in the reactor was gone, corium had melted through the reactor vessel, and the primary containment had been breached.

Three hours after the explosion at unit 1, the Japanese government had doubled the evacuation zone around the plant to 12.4 miles. But for those at the plant, evacuation wasn't possible.

—⌂—

The unthinkable had already happened—a nuclear reactor had melted down. But operators still needed to find a way to get water into the reactor at unit 1. Unless they could cool the mass of corium, the chain reaction would continue unchecked, growing hotter and hotter until the corium ate through the concrete of the secondary containment. And they had five other reactors to keep an eye on, too. Workers had been sleeping at the plant, cycling in and out of the control rooms and repair teams in shifts. Many feared they were putting themselves in mortal danger to save the power plant, but they were determined to protect their families and all the people living in the surrounding towns. They went about their work with the grim resolve of soldiers in battle.

One worker later described taking off his wedding ring before his shift because he feared it would be contaminated with radiation and have to be left behind. But then he thought better of it—he knew that if something happened to him, his body could be identified by the ring. So he put it back on. Another worker remembered calling his father before his shift and asking him to take care of his wife and daughter if he died.

Operators wore radiation suits for protection. The suit's function is to prevent radioactive dust from hitching a ride on the wearer's body—in their hair or clothes, on their skin, or in their lungs. But the fabric of a radiation suit cannot block the kind of radiation that comes from a reactor. Even with protective gear, the workers were exposed.

To make matters worse, the plant's store of alarm pocket dosimeters, which let out a high-pitched two-tone alarm if the radiation level climbs too quickly, was largely wiped out by the tsunami. Usually, anyone working near radiation would be required to carry this potentially lifesaving device. Instead, only the leader of each operational team was given one.

Following the explosion in unit 1, operators in the control room next to it didn't have a lot of options to reduce their radiation exposure. There was no shield between the control room and the radiation that had escaped containment. They simply didn't have the option to leave the control room and reduce the length of their exposure. The best they could manage was to move to the unit 2 side of the building when they didn't need to be at the instruments and crouch down—adding a little distance between themselves and the radiation source and reducing their height so they presented less surface area to be hit by radiation.

Despite the explosion, operators for unit 1 needed to press forward with their efforts to cool the reactor. No one could be sure what, exactly, was going on inside it. They only knew that they needed to get water into the reactor core to prevent the chain reaction from spiraling out of control. A fire engine had already managed to pump more than 20,000 gallons of water into the reactor at unit 1. But by 2:53 that afternoon, less than an hour before the explosion, they had run out of fresh water to inject. Desperate to replace the cooling water in the reactor, Yoshida decided it was time to try his last resort: seawater.

Normally, nuclear reactors use purified water, which runs through a closed system to ensure that none of the water from the reactor can get out—and that no impurities can get in. That's because minerals in unpurified water can attach to the metal surfaces and fuel rods in the reactor core, interfering with the carefully maintained reaction occurring inside. The salt in seawater also corrodes metal and destroys electrical connectors. (That was why the plant's backup generators had failed after they were flooded by the tsunami.) Everyone knew the injection of seawater would damage the reactor beyond repair. But they had no choice—nothing was more important than getting water around the overheating fuel rods.

In order to span the distance from the seawater holding tank, three fire trucks needed to be connected by a series of hoses to form a chain. In the hours before the explosion, workers had laid out fire hoses in preparation for the seawater injection, but those had been damaged by the blast. They needed to be repaired or replaced.

Fire trucks, photographed on March 16 among tsunami and explosion debris on the Fukushima Daiichi grounds, were used to pump seawater into the reactors.

Workers scrambled to get the pumping system back online, patching the hoses that could be salvaged and cobbling together any new hoses they could find to replace the ones that could not. It was past 7:00 P.M. before they started pumping seawater into the reactor. But in the meantime, Prime Minister Naoto Kan had balked at the idea. Not fully versed on the workings of the reactor, he was concerned that the seawater could lead to another explosion. The drastic measure would also send a clear message to the outside world that TEPCO had given up on the idea that unit 1 could be saved.

Kan pressured TEPCO to stop the seawater injection. But Yoshida worried that the odds of getting their ad hoc pumping system going again would be slim if they stopped. He also knew that injecting the seawater was their only hope of keeping the chain reaction in unit 1 from reaching a point of no return, and that every minute counted. So he hatched a plan to keep the seawater flowing. He took one of his workers aside and told him that, on a video conference call with TEPCO headquarters, he was going to order the workers to stop the seawater injection . . . but he wanted them to ignore the order.

It was a gutsy move. Yoshida was not only lying to his bosses at TEPCO, he was also defying an order from the prime minister of Japan. But he knew that nothing was more important than getting water into the melting core.

The call went as planned; the seawater injection continued.

Workers in the main control room for units 3 and 4 had noticed a sudden climb in radiation in their workspace after the hydrogen explosion in unit 1 the day before, but they didn't have the luxury of evacuating. They had their own problems to deal with.

After the earthquake, reactor 3 had scrammed, triggering the RCIC system to keep cooling water flowing through the reactor. All had gone well until the morning after the tsunami, when the RCIC had shut down. An emergency injection system, or HPCI (pronounced "Hipsy"), had automatically kicked in when the RCIC shut down around noon on March 12. Because they had battery power, water injection had been a far easier task for the operators of unit 3 than it was for those of unit 1, but they were still improvising. The HPCI was meant to be used in the case of a sudden loss of water, like when a pipe ruptures. It delivered far more water than the RCIC system, and operators had to constantly monitor the flow.

Despite the demands it placed on the operators, the HPCI had kept the core cool. But in the early morning light of March 13, the HPCI also appeared to be failing. Operators decided they would have to try to use fire hoses to deliver water to the core. But this solution was short-lived. Not long after the fire hoses began pumping, the batteries powering unit 3 sputtered out.

In an echo of the events at unit 1, pressure in the unit 3 reactor began to climb as operators tried to open a safety release valve and vent steam. It was 8:41 A.M. before they were successful. And it was too little, too late: At around 9:00, the water in the reactor sank below the tops of the fuel rods.

By 10:40, the core was melting down.

—⁀ᶺ⌢—

It was two days after the earthquake, and the bad news kept coming. Both the Fukushima Daiichi and Fukushima Daini plants were out of commission following the tsunami, creating a shortage in the electricity supply. TEPCO announced a series of rolling blackouts throughout central Japan. Necessities of all kinds were also in short supply near the stricken coast. Fuel became scarce, and emergency supplies such as water and batteries had flown off store shelves. Ninety-six aftershocks shook the island on the 13th, causing more damage and anxiety.

Even worse, all along the northeastern coast of Japan, bodies began to wash up on shore. More than two thousand would be found by the morning of March 14.

But help began to trickle in, too: 100,000 troops from the Japan Civil Defense forces arrived in Tohoku, along with trucks carrying drinking water and food. Search-and-rescue teams combed the wreckage for survivors and bodies. And the first helicopters cut in from the ocean, carrying emergency supplies from a fleet of American ships offshore.

Two days after the tsunami, tens of thousands of people were still missing. Residents in Natori, a town in Miyagi Prefecture, posted notes hoping that family members would read them and be reunited.

radioactive cloud

Monday, March 14, 2011

Reactor Status

    Reactor 1: Melted down/building destroyed
    Reactor 2: Scrammed
    Reactor 3: Melted down
    Reactor 4: Shut down
    Reactor 5: Shut down
    Reactor 6: Shut down

Two hundred and seven miles away from Fukushima Daiichi, the USS *Ronald Reagan* was standing by in the North Pacific Ocean. A U.S. Navy aircraft carrier more than 1,092 feet long and carrying about 3,200 crew members, it had been on its way to South Korea to participate in naval maneuvers when the earthquake hit Japan. It received new orders to join a relief effort called Operation *Tomodachi*. (*Tomodachi* means "friendship.")

With supply routes on land severely damaged, the quickest route for bringing humanitarian supplies such as food, water, and first-aid equipment to devastated coastal towns was by sea, so the aircraft carrier headed for Japan, where it would serve as a fueling and supply station for disaster relief operations. The

Reagan was moving fast, but as it neared Sendai, the sea became thick with wreckage from the tsunami. The ship slowed to a crawl. Lindsay Cooper, a petty officer third class on the aircraft carrier, later remembered, "You could hardly see the water. All you saw was wood, trees, and boats. The ship stopped moving because there was so much debris." When the tsunami waves receded, they had dragged the rubble of the Japanese coastal

An aerial photo taken from a U.S. Navy helicopter on March 12 shows timber and rubble swept out to sea by the tsunami.

communities they had devastated—buildings, telephone poles, cars, and even people—with them.

But tsunami debris wasn't the only danger off the coast. The ship took a position at what was considered a safe distance from Fukushima Daiichi—100 miles. They soon discovered that they needed to be farther away.

A nuclear-powered ship, the *Reagan* was equipped with radiation sensors. On the morning of the 13th, sensors in the engine room had registered radiation levels on deck at more than twice normal. That same day, three helicopters that flew on a mission closer to the plant had returned to the ship covered in radioactive dust.

Seventeen crew members who had ridden in the helicopters

Sailors aboard the USS *Ronald Reagan* scrub down the ship's decks to remove any radioactive particles that may have accumulated.

had to be decontaminated, scrubbed from head to foot to remove any radioactive particles. Their clothes were sealed in plastic bags for disposal.

Sailors on the *Reagan* later reported that they had been caught in a radioactive cloud. A senior chief petty officer named Angel Torres remembered, "All of the sudden, this big cloud engulfs us. It wasn't white smoke. It was like something I'd never seen before."

Lindsay Cooper remembered not how the cloud looked, but how it felt. A gust of warm air blew across the ship's deck, cutting through the falling snow. "Almost immediately, I felt like my nose was bleeding," she said. It wasn't, but the air smelled and tasted metallic, like blood.

The *Reagan* had run afoul of nuclear power's thorniest problem: radioactive isotopes.

As sources of electricity go, nuclear fission is incredibly efficient. A single uranium pellet, just half an inch across, can produce the same amount of energy as 1 ton of coal or 149 barrels of oil. And while burning a ton of coal in a properly functioning coal-burning plant releases more than 2 tons of carbon dioxide (one of the gases that contributes to global climate change), a nuclear reactor releases none. But nuclear fission does create waste, in the form of radioactive isotopes.

When an atom of uranium splits, the pieces aren't just smaller than the original atoms; they also have a different number of protons in their nuclei. That means that the new atoms are no longer uranium—they have become different elements. And they aren't necessarily stable.

Elements are defined by the number of protons in their nucleus—all oxygen atoms have eight, and if an atom has six protons, it's carbon—but the number of neutrons can vary. Atoms of the same element that have different numbers of neutrons are called isotopes of each other. If the number of neutrons creates an imbalance in the atom's nucleus, that isotope is radioactive. Over time, it will shed neutrons, protons, or both until it reaches a more stable form. As the neutrons and protons fly the coop, they travel as radiation.

Exactly when any given atom will shed its loose particles is anyone's guess. Scientists talk about the life of an isotope in terms of probability. Imagine that you've been put in charge of ten energetic kindergartners. You sit them all on a rug, crisscross applesauce, and tell them to stay seated. You can't predict exactly when each kid will pop up from his or her seat. But you know that at some point, they all will. If you've done this before, you probably know that the wiggliest kid can only keep their butt on the carpet for about thirty seconds. The calmest one will make it to ten minutes. Based on that range, you can predict that about half of the kids will be up and running around in about five minutes.

Determining when a radioactive isotope will decay—shed those extra neutrons and protons—is similar. Rather than saying exactly how long it will be before a specific atom decays, scientists give the amount of time it will take for half of any group of atoms in a particular isotope to decay. If an isotope is said to have a half-life of five years, you can expect roughly half of the atoms to have decayed in that amount of time. Of the remaining atoms, half of those will decay in the next five years.

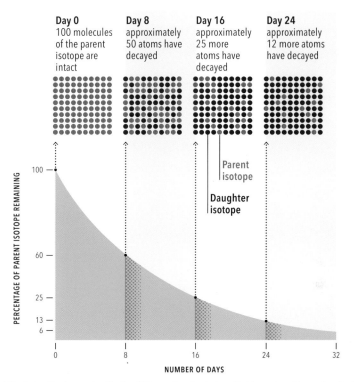

Day 0	Day 8	Day 16	Day 24
100 molecules of the parent isotope are intact	approximately 50 atoms have decayed	approximately 25 more atoms have decayed	approximately 12 more atoms have decayed

Parent isotope

Daughter isotope

PERCENTAGE OF PARENT ISOTOPE REMAINING

100

60

25

13
6

0   8   16   24   32

NUMBER OF DAYS

This chart illustrates the decay rate of iodine 131, a radioactive isotope that is produced by nuclear fission. It has a half-life of 8 days, which means that after 24 days, there would be about 14% of the original iodine left. It would take about 56 days for the levels of remaining radioactive iodine to reach less than 1%.

A nuclear power plant that is humming along properly contains its radiation in the reactor. In an accident, radiation—the protons and neutrons that continue to fly from the broken halves of uranium in the fuel—may travel a short distance from the reactor. But radioactive isotopes—the broken bits themselves—can travel far from their source. Carried in smoke and steam, they drift on the wind or in the water. Eventually, they decay, emitting radiation in their new location. The impact of that decay isn't much of an issue unless the atom happens to be on or in a living body when it breaks down. There, the radiation emitted by a decaying isotope will strike one of the body's cells.

Nuclear operators go through rigorous control measures to make sure they don't carry radioactive dust out of the plant at the end of a workday. Anyone working in an area where radioactive materials may have been is required to wear a radiation suit—usually coveralls that are fastened tightly at the ankles and wrists, gloves, special socks, boots, goggles, and a breathing mask with a filter. Without the suit, bits of dust containing

Hood
Protects hair and connects seamlessly to jumpsuit so that no particles can enter around the neck.

Face mask

Tyvek jumpsuit
Provides complete coverage over clothes. Ankles and wrists should be taped closed to prevent particles from getting in.

Gloves
Overlap sleeves.

High rubber boots
Overlap pant legs.

Plastic overshoes
Can be easily removed upon leaving an exposed area to avoid tracking materials on boot soles

radioactive isotopes could cling to clothes and hair, and might be inhaled or swallowed.

Control room operators at Daiichi were wearing full gear, but the airtight radiation suits weren't made for long-term use. They were hot and uncomfortable and simply impossible to keep intact over long periods of time. And the workers had to eat and drink. To do that, they had to pull off their face masks. It was a major breach of safety protocol that risked the workers swallowing radioactive dust with their food or inhaling it while they ate. But it was that or starve. In a situation where every moment counted, they could not take the time to leave the control room and eat in a safer environment.

Workers at the plant were being exposed to high levels of radiation, and it became clear they wouldn't be able to stay within the legal exposure limit. By law, Japanese nuclear workers could not be exposed to more than 50 mSv of radiation per year. In emergency situations, the limit went up to 100 mSv per year. The law protected workers by making sure they didn't receive doses of radiation that were unsafe. To stay within the legal limit, the workers needed to leave the plant if they reached that dose, and they were desperately needed where they were. So on March 14, Japan's Ministry of Health, Labor, and Welfare raised the legal limit for annual exposure in an emergency to 250 mSv.

It's incredibly difficult to say how much damage a radioactive isotope will do in the human body. Large doses can cause acute radiation sickness. But at smaller doses, the results are less certain. In the end, the damage done comes down to chance. While radiation has a very real power to damage cells, the most likely effect of that damage is cell death. In small numbers, the loss of cells is not a serious threat. Our body constantly generates new cells to replace old and damaged ones. But in some cases, radiation may strike a cell's DNA. Remember how ionizing radiation breaks apart the bonds in molecules? Each spiraling ladder of your DNA is a single, amazingly complex molecule. If one of the bonds in its DNA is affected, the cell is likely to repair the damage. But if it cannot, the error will affect the way the cell reproduces. The result, in that case, can be cancer. No one knows whether any one exposure will be the unlucky one that starts disease. But one thing is certain: the more radiation a person is exposed to, the greater the odds that it will strike a cell's DNA. At higher levels of exposure, the probability of a worker later developing cancer begins to climb.

In order to do harm, a radioactive isotope must be in or on the body when it decays. That means that breathing in or swallowing a radioactive isotope poses the greatest danger. But what if a radioactive isotope *is* swallowed? Our bodies are incredibly picky. During digestion, a body only retains the elements that are useful to it. And it only holds on to radioactive isotopes if they are similar to elements it needs. Nuclear fission creates several isotopes that are close enough to minerals the body needs to be dangerous. Strontium 90 is chemically similar to calcium, and so it is absorbed by the body and deposited in the bones. Once there, it can remain for decades, releasing radiation into the bones and bone marrow. Cesium 137 behaves like potassium and is used throughout the body, winding up mostly in muscle tissue. Iodine 131 resembles naturally occurring iodine 127, which concentrates in the thyroid gland.

But if the body doesn't need a nutrient at the time that it is taken in, it won't absorb it. Iodine 131 is a particularly problematic radioactive isotope because it tends to drift for long distances on the wind. But in the event of a nuclear accident, people who may be exposed to iodine 131 can take potassium iodide tablets, which provide enough non-radioactive iodine 127 to saturate the thyroid. The body, no longer needing iodine, will simply let any radioactive iodine it may encounter pass through harmlessly.

Children evacuated from the area around Fukushima Daiichi are given potassium iodide pills to protect against the absorption of radioactive iodine 131 on March 14.

—∿—

As the reactors melted down at Fukushima Daiichi, workers in and around the plant took regular readings to determine how much radioactivity had escaped. They weren't the only ones.

Twenty-five years earlier, another reactor had melted down near Chernobyl, Ukraine. Cows living near the Chernobyl plant had grazed on grass covered in iodine 131. Children, who are particularly vulnerable to the effects of iodine 131, had drunk the cows' milk. Many later developed thyroid cancer.

The contamination had reached far beyond the area surrounding the Chernobyl reactor; radioactive isotopes had also spread across Europe. Cesium 137 rained down more than a thousand miles away in Scotland, where it covered fields and wound up being concentrated in the flesh of livestock.

Four years after the Chernobyl disaster, the International Atomic Energy Agency (IAEA) developed a scale called the International Nuclear and Radiological Event Scale (INES) to rate the impact of nuclear accidents. Much like the moment magnitude scale, each number on the INES scale, which runs from 1 to 7, indicates an impact that is ten times worse than the number before it. A nuclear accident that occurred at Three Mile Island in Pennsylvania in 1979 was classified after the fact as a level 5. At the time of the Fukushima events, Chernobyl was the only accident to ever rate a level 7.

Now scientists from the IAEA were carefully monitoring radiation readings in the areas around Fukushima. They feared that Fukushima might become a repeat of the accident at Chernobyl. Radiation readings from the USS *Ronald Reagan*

International Nuclear Event Scale

● Incident   ● Accident

Ines **1**	Anomaly	Minor problem with safety components at a nuclear facility, but significant safety margin remaining
Ines **2**	Incident	Minor exposure of a member of the public, contamination within the facility, significant failures without consequences to plant safety
Ines **3**	Serious incident	Exposure to workers greater than ten times legal limit, near-accident with no further safety margin remaining, severe plant contamination
Ines **4**	Accident with local consequences	High probability of radioactive release, significant fuel damage, at least one death from radiation
Ines **5**	Accident with wider consequences	High probability of public exposure, severe damage to core, multiple deaths from radiation
Ines **6**	Serious accident	Significant release of radioactive material, likely to require countermeasures
Ines **7**	Major accident	Major release with widespread health and environmental impacts

confirmed that radioactive isotopes had already blown miles out to sea.

When large amounts of radioactive isotopes are released into the air, as they were during the explosion at reactor 1, they can form a radioactive cloud of isotopes mixed with air, smoke, water, and other particles from the explosion. Like rain clouds, radiation clouds are driven by the weather. The same air currents that blow storms across the ocean and onto land push radioactive gases, too. The Comprehensive Nuclear-Test-Ban Treaty Organization, which monitors releases of radioactive isotopes around the world, was also watching the unfolding disaster on the eastern coast of Japan. The group created a weather-based map that showed the likely path of the radioactive plume from Fukushima swirling across the North Pacific and sweeping onto the west coast of the United States.

—⋀—

Operators at the Fukushima Daiichi plant didn't have time to think about the radiation drifting over the Pacific. They were caught in a seemingly endless cycle of emergencies. It had been three days since the tsunami, and conditions at the plant continued to grow worse. Hydrogen gas had been leaking into the unit 3 building since the day before. They had managed to vent the reactor vessel four times after the fuel began melting. They knew that if the gas built up, the containment building was likely to explode, just as unit 1 had. But an explosion in unit 3 would be much worse. The building had reinforced concrete walls on the upper floor, making it a sturdier structure that would be able to hold more gas before the system failed. The stronger structure might buy them more time, but it also meant that an even larger cloud of flammable gas was building up.

Fears of another explosion made it difficult to work. Supervisors had to balance the need to save the reactor against the safety of their workers. "We alternated between deploying and pulling back workers, because we were afraid of another hydrogen explosion," Takeyuki Inagaki remembered.

On the morning of the 14th, they brainstormed ways to open up the unit 3 building to let out hydrogen steam. But they were too late. At 11:01 A.M., a hydrogen explosion bigger and more violent than the one they had experienced two days earlier rocked

The explosion in the unit 3 building completely destroyed its concrete walls.

unit 3. The blast sent a cloud of black smoke, thick with concrete dust, hundreds of feet into the air. Massive hunks of concrete rained down around the building.

About fifty workers who were near the building scrambled for cover. The members of a team that had been working inside the building at unit 2 were shocked, when they came out, to discover that the car they had used to reach the building had been blown away by the force of the blast. Chunks of the unit 3 building littered roads around the complex, making it even harder to get around.

When Inagaki remembered the moment years later for a television interview, tears filled his eyes. "Since there were so many people out there, I was really afraid for their safety. I thought to myself, *It's very possible someone was killed*," he said. "Then, one by one, people started to trickle back. They were all very pale in the face and some were bleeding." Eleven workers were injured in the explosion, but all of them had survived.

The supervisors' relief was short-lived. After accounting for the crew that had been outside during the explosion, they turned back to their instruments and discovered that the water level in unit 2 had started to go down. The disastrous meltdown cycle was about to begin again.

At this point, the workers had been struggling relentlessly for days, with very little sleep. One worker later remembered, "What was happening was beyond what we trained for on a daily basis. Using what little information we had, we had to decide immediately what we'd do . . . It was a race against time."

Takeyuki Inagaki put it this way: "From the fourteenth to early in the morning on the fifteenth . . . it was like being in hell."

Every task was critical, the stakes life-and-death. And despite their best efforts and the endless hours of work, they were losing the race. The reactors were melting down, one by one.

The explosion in unit 3 had badly shaken the workers, many of whom had barely escaped with their lives. Now Superintendent Yoshida had to beg them to go back into danger to try to save unit 2.

Once all of the heads been counted and they were sure no one had been killed in the explosion, Yoshida sent workers who had been injured in the blast to another site where they could be treated. Then he gathered the remaining crew together. "Everybody was in a daze and could hardly think," he later remembered. He called the workers together and took responsibility for having sent them into the line of fire, saying his judgment was to blame. Then he made a difficult request. He asked workers to go back out onto the grounds and clear away the highly radioactive rubble that surrounded Reactor 2.

Of the three reactors that had been operating when the tsunami hit, unit 2 was the only one that was still intact. It had been functioning pretty well, but around noon on March 14, that had begun to change. Just as it had in reactors 1 and 3, the water in reactor 2 boiled off and pressure in the reactor vessel began to climb. But while they had eventually managed to vent some steam from the other two reactors, operators were unable to vent unit 2 at all. And that meant that they couldn't get any water in.

"We had come to a situation where [nuclear] fuel was really exposed, but we could not lower pressure or pump in water," Yoshida remembered. "I thought then, though not for the first time, that we were going to die. I thought we were really going to die. With no water coming in, the number 2 reactor was going to melt. All fuel was going to really override pressure in the containment vessel and escape outside. That would have been a worst-case accident." Yoshida knew that a meltdown of that magnitude would be catastrophic. If the containment layers at unit 2 were destroyed, it would be too dangerous for workers to continue pumping water into units 1 and 3. All three of the reactors would be completely out of control.

The water in reactor 2 fell below the tops of the fuel rods by 5:00 P.M. By 7:20, the core began to melt.

The race was over. All three of the active reactors at Fukushima Daiichi had melted down.

DAY 5

fukushima 50

Tuesday, March 15, 2011

Reactor Status

    Reactor 1: Melted down, building destroyed
    Reactor 2: Melted down
    Reactor 3: Melted down, building destroyed
    Reactor 4: Building destroyed
    Reactor 5: Shut down
    Reactor 6: Shut down

The three active reactors at Fukushima had broken down, one after another, following the same pattern. Now that unit 2 was clearly in trouble, operators figured it was only a matter of time before the building surrounding it, like the ones that housed units 1 and 3, exploded. So they weren't overly surprised when, at 6:12 on Tuesday morning, a loud rumble shook the control room.

Everyone in the emergency response center assumed there had been a hydrogen gas explosion in the unit 2 building. But the explosion was actually in an entirely unexpected place: the unit 4 building.

As it turned out, unit 2 had caught a lucky break when unit 1 had blown. The force of that blast had knocked a square panel from unit 2's exterior, creating a vent for the hydrogen gas building up inside. A cloud of white steam had been pouring from the side of the building since then, preventing the buildup that had been so disastrous in the other two buildings.

The leak may have saved unit 2 from explosion, but it was also releasing radioactivity into the air. And in the early hours of Tuesday morning, the favorable winds that had been sweeping the radioactive gases out to sea had shifted, carrying radioactive cesium inland.

A man named Toru Anzai, who lived in the town of Iitate, a full 25 miles northwest of the Fukushima plant, later remembered the explosion at reactor 4. "I heard the sound of the explosion, and the air turned hazy and rust-red. There was also a metallic burning smell, and even indoors my face and exposed skin started to sting. The radiation was very high around that time. My legs felt as though they were sunburned." That night, a radiation monitor at the village hall in Iitate registered 44.7 mSv per hour. Remember, the legal limit for radiation exposure for a worker in emergency situations had just been raised from 100 to 250 mSv *per year*. With radiation levels at 44.7 mSv per hour, people would reach the emergency exposure maximum in less than six hours.

A radiation-monitoring car parked at the plant's gates, two-thirds of a mile from reactor 4, had been taking readings regularly since March 11. On the morning of March 15, radiation levels spiked to 12 mSv per hour. At that rate, workers would exceed 250 mSv of exposure in less than a day. It was no longer safe for workers to stay in the control rooms near the reactors— or anywhere outside the emergency response center.

The emergency response team debated whether to evacuate

the plant. Yoshida told his crew to prepare vehicles in case an evacuation was necessary, and to find temporary shelter on the grounds of Fukushima Daiichi. But in the confusion of the moment his command was garbled, and nearly 650 workers clambered onto buses and immediately evacuated to Fukushima Daini, about 6 miles away. Superintendent Yoshida and a team of about seventy supervisors stayed behind to keep fighting.

For Yoshida, abandoning the premises was not an option. Leaving the plant without any workers would cause a major catastrophe—one far worse than the three explosions that had already happened. But that left him with the grim task of determining which employees were essential and asking them to stay. "It was like deciding who would die with me," he later recalled. "The faces of my team appeared before me one after another . . . I couldn't bear the idea that these people I had known for years might die on my orders," Yoshida recalled, "but I knew that our only hope was to keep injecting water. I had no choice. I had to ask them to prepare for the worst."

The plant workers who stayed were driven by a sense of duty. Nuclear engineer Atsufumi Yoshizawa had been working from a disaster-response station about 3 miles from the plant. When he and some of his coworkers volunteered to return to Fukushima Daiichi, they filed past a line of firefighters, policemen, and other employees who saluted them. "We felt like members of the Tokkotai," he later said, referring to Japanese kamikaze pilots during World War II. "The people lined up outside never said as much, but I could tell by their expressions that they didn't think we would return."

Yet the workers were determined. "We knew that we would not be replaced," Yoshizawa remembered. "No one was forced to stay, but those of us who remained knew that we would be there until the end. We knew that we were the only people capable of saving the plant."

—⟋⟍—

The explosion in unit 4 had caused the top two floors of the building to collapse and sent workers who had been out on the grounds cleaning up the radioactive debris left by the first two explosions scurrying for safety. Dressed in full radiation suits, they headed for the emergency response center. It was not an easy trip. The roads between the reactor and the seismic isolated building were choked with debris from the explosions. The workers' protective suits restricted their movement, and it was almost two

The explosion in the unit 4 building collapsed its top floors and destroyed equipment on other levels.

hours before they reached the emergency response center. Until then, Superintendent Yoshida had no idea that the explosion they had heard that morning had actually come from unit 4.

He received the news with dismay. Because the reactor at unit 4 had been shut down when the tsunami swept in, it seemed likely that the explosion had come from a spent fuel pool. And that was a nuclear disaster of a whole different kind.

_⌁_

The fuel pellets that drive the chain reaction in a nuclear reactor are not particularly radioactive. About 95 percent of each pellet is uranium 238, an isotope with a half-life of 4.5 billion years. The rest is uranium 235, which has a half-life of 704 million years. That means that the atoms in the fuel are much, much, *much* slower to decay than, say, the atoms in iodine 131, which has a half-life of eight days. The pellets of uranium will be as old as Earth is now before half of the uranium 238 atoms have emitted radiation. To put it simply: They are safe enough to be handled with bare hands.

Once uranium atoms have been struck by neutrons and fissioned, however, it is a completely different matter. In a reactor, many of the uranium 235 nuclei split apart, transforming into radioactive isotopes such as iodine 131 and cesium 137. Some of the uranium 238 atoms will absorb a stray neutron and undergo a series of transformations to become plutonium 239.

As the uranium 235 atoms in the fuel are split, their numbers begin to dwindle. It becomes less likely that a neutron will strike a uranium 235 nucleus, and the fuel can no longer sustain a chain reaction. At that point, the fuel is considered spent. The rods must be removed from the reactor and stored. But they are still highly radioactive, loaded with radioactive isotopes, the by-products of fission.

Each of the reactor buildings at Fukushima Daiichi included a massive spent fuel pool on the fifth floor. The smallest pool, in unit 1, held 261,000 gallons of water. The largest, in unit 6, held more than 385,000—a little more than half the volume of an Olympic-sized pool.

When it was time to store the fuel from one of the reactors at Fukushima Daiichi, operators would bring the reactor to cold shutdown. They would flood the entire fifth floor of the building with water. A crane could then carry the spent fuel through the water to the storage pool, keeping the fuel rods submerged the whole time. The excess water would later be drained off.

The fuel pools were designed to provide maximum shielding: Each was made of 5-foot-thick concrete with a steel liner. Although the top of the pool was open, the rods were covered by at least 23 feet of water at all times.

Just like the water that cooled the reactor, the water in the

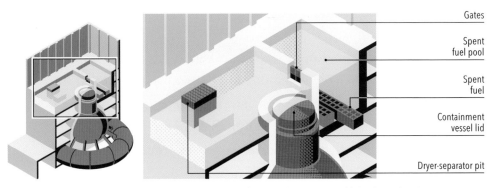

In order to move spent fuel, nuclear operators must first bring the reactor to cold shutdown. Then the reactor core and spent fuel storage are flooded with enough water to submerge the area to a depth of about 30 feet. Rods remain submerged in the coolant and radiation shield of the water while they are being moved.

spent fuel pools did double duty. It provided a shield, preventing radiation from escaping, and it also cooled the rods. Although mostly spent, the rods could still produce decay heat. A cooling system kept the water surrounding the fuel rods in the storage pools below 95°F.

Before the tsunami, units 4, 5, and 6 had been shut down for maintenance. Units 5 and 6 still had fuel in their reactors, but they were in cold shutdown. They also still had power, so the water level and temperature inside each reactor could be monitored. In unit 4, however, the fuel from the reactor had already been transferred to the storage pool. That meant the pool had more spent fuel than the others. And since it had only recently been removed from the reactor, the fuel was hotter, too.

When the plant lost power, operators had known that the spent fuel pools were in peril, but they also knew that they had some time to solve the problem. The shaking from the earthquakes and explosions had sloshed about 3 feet of water from each, but that still left hundreds of thousands of gallons in the pools. In unit 4, the entire fifth floor was still flooded from the fuel-removal process. By the emergency team's calculations, they had at least a week before enough water would be lost to cause trouble, so they had focused on more pressing problems.

But all that changed when the unit 4 operators arrived at the command center with news of its explosion. Radiation levels near the building had soared to 400 mSv an hour—a dose high enough to be deadly after several hours' exposure. They knew a fire was burning inside the unit, but no one could get close enough to see where it was. Everything pointed to the possibility that the fuel in the spent pool was no longer underwater, and that the zirconium cladding that encased the fuel rods had ignited.

There was one major difference between the fuel in the spent storage pools and the fuel inside the reactors. The nuclear reactors were encased in containment vessels that kept most of the radiation from escaping in case of an accident. The storage pools, loaded with a total of almost 900 tons of spent fuel, had no containment structures. In the cases of units 3 and 4, there was no longer even a roof over them. If there really was a fire in one of the storage pools, there was nothing to hold in radioactive materials, which would be carried in the smoke. Even worse, the heat generated could create an updraft, carrying any radiation that was released high into the atmosphere, where it could travel for miles before coming back down.

Both TEPCO and the Japanese government were concerned about causing panic among the population. In public statements, they tried to walk a fine line between keeping people informed about radiation leaks that could affect them and holding back details so people wouldn't experience unnecessary fear.

But news agencies had been filming Fukushima Daiichi from the air almost continuously since the slow-motion accident had begun. Attempts to reassure people that things were under control were undermined by footage of units 1 and 3 belching smoke. Videos of the explosions ran continuously on television and online, and the efforts of the skeleton crew at the plant captured imaginations around the world. Although there were seventy workers, the media called them the Fukushima 50.

Travelers in Seoul, South Korea, which is across the Sea of Japan and about 750 miles away from the plant, watch television news coverage of the Fukushima Disaster on March 16, 2011.

The reduced crew at Fukushima Daiichi was scrambling to understand and control the situation. They had very little information to work with. But the government and news organizations outside the plant had even less.

Around the world, experts tried to piece together the fragments of information they did have in order to form a picture of what was happening. It didn't look good. The crisis was at its peak, with three reactors melting down and an additional building in flames.

At about the same time as the explosion in unit 4, operators in the unit 2 control room had thought they heard another explosion coming from the torus beneath reactor 2. A malfunctioning gauge in the torus had shown a sudden drop in pressure. They assumed that the torus had ruptured—meaning that the containment vessel for the reactor had been breached.

The possibility of a containment breach in unit 2 combined

with a meltdown in the unit 4 fuel pool was a radiological nightmare. A senior reactor engineering specialist at the Research Reactor Institute at Kyoto University, Hiroaki Koide, was interviewed by *The New York Times* that day. "We are on the brink," he said. "We are now facing the worst-case scenario."

—◡〜◡—

Officials at the Nuclear Regulatory Commission in the United States had the same thought. They ran simulations and realized that a breach in the unit 2 torus combined with a meltdown in the unit 4 fuel pool would require everyone within a 50-mile radius of the plant—more than 2 million people—to evacuate. Privately, Prime Minister Naoto Kan worried that the fuel in all six of the fuel pools might melt. A meltdown of that size could require the evacuation of Tokyo—a city of more than 13 million. "If Tokyo needed to be evacuated," he later said, "I feared the entire nation of Japan would be paralyzed by chaos for quite a long time."

Some residents of Tokyo decided not to wait. They packed their bags and headed out of town. Many people living outside the evacuation zone in Fukushima decided to err on the side of caution, too. The government had issued an order for people living beyond the evacuation zone of 12 miles but within 19 miles of the plant to remain inside with their windows and doors closed, and helicopters and airplanes were banned from flying over the site. Many people feared they might be trapped in their homes if conditions worsened, so they opted to leave instead. They may have had the right idea. That night, radiation fell from the clouds in a flurry of rain and snow, endangering the residents of towns that weren't in the evacuation zone.

Evacuees at a shelter about 40 miles from Fukushima Daiichi on March 18.

Gasoline supplies petered out. Suppliers were reluctant to drive near the evacuation zones, so no more would be coming. Still, a stream of refugees made their way to Yamagata, the prefecture west of Fukushima, where they would sleep on floors in crowded gymnasiums and municipal buildings.

At the plant, all eyes turned to the steaming buildings of units 3 and 4. Operators needed to get water into the fuel pools, but the pools were five stories in the air, and there was no way to access them from below. A plan to have Special Defense Forces helicopters drop water on the reactors was scuttled when it became clear that radiation levels above the reactors were too high for helicopter pilots to safely do the job. As night fell, the picture looked grim.

turning point

Wednesday, March 16, 2011

```
Reactor Status
    Reactor 1: Melted down, building destroyed
    Reactor 2: Melted down
    Reactor 3: Melted down, building destroyed
    Reactor 4: Building destroyed
    Reactor 5: Shut down
    Reactor 6: Shut down
```

On Wednesday, the U.S. ambassador to Japan, John V. Roos, issued a recommendation that all American citizens living within 50 miles of the plant evacuate. The announcement did little to settle the fears of Japanese citizens, who had been told to evacuate only up to 12 miles from Fukushima Daiichi. The governor of Fukushima, Yuhei Sato, said, "Anxiety and anger felt by people have reached boiling point."

It didn't help that another fire had broken out at the unit 4 reactor, and attempts to reach the fuel pools by helicopter that morning were once again stymied by radiation. The copters did manage to drop some water onto the buildings, but they were forced to fly so high that very little made it to their targets.

Despite their inability to add water to the pools, the helicopter flights marked a change in fortune for the workers at the plant. The night before, they had been sure that the spent fuel pools were on the brink of disaster. But as the light of a new day shone into the reactor buildings, they saw an entirely different picture. Although the helicopter had to stay high above the reactors, skirting the areas of extremely high radiation directly above them, operators on board saw a glimmer of something in the spent fuel pool for unit 4—a snippet of sky, reflected on the surface of the water.

A properly filled spent fuel pool at Fukushima Daiichi, photographed before the disaster.

There was water in the pools. It was impossible to say how much was there, but the nightmare scenario, that the fuel was dry and burning, had not turned out to be true.

The hydrogen explosion in unit 4 had had nothing to do with the spent fuel pool. The building shared a smokestack with unit 3. When hydrogen had built up in the unit 3 building, it had backed up into unit 4, too, and been sparked into an explosion in the air ducts on the building's fourth floor. The fires, which had been caused by oil spilled on the floor, burned out on their own.

Eventually, the plant operators realized that the worst-case scenario in unit 2—that the torus had exploded and was leaking—hadn't happened, either. Much later, investigators would realize that faulty readings from the broken gauge accompanied by the sound of the explosion from unit 4 had led operators to the wrong conclusion.

Although the crisis would drag on for long weeks and months after March 16, the operators had reached a turning point. There would be no further explosions to undo their work. Seawater was being pumped into the reactors at units 1, 2, and 3, pulling them farther from the brink of destruction every day.

Anxious to stabilize the spent fuel pools, operators ran four more helicopter flights on the evening of March 17, but radiation levels above the reactors were still too high. The helicopters had to fly too far above the reactor buildings, and the strong March winds carried most of the water they dropped—about 6,000 pounds in all—away from their targets.

On the night of March 18, a team of elite firefighters from Tokyo arrived with fire trucks designed to put out fires in skyscrapers. Seasoned professionals who were trained to navigate towering fires in the skyscrapers of Tokyo, they were nevertheless visibly shaken by the challenge of working close to the open reactor pools. "The plan was to get water into unit 3 by any means necessary," deputy fire chief Yukio Takayama later recounted. Their target was five stories over their heads and hidden from view, but they had to hit the pools dead-on. And they needed to do it quickly. "Two thoughts kept running through my mind," Takayama remembered. *"Please be over soon,* and *What will I do if this place explodes?* I had never felt that kind of fear before. I thought, *This is what it feels like to really be in trouble."*

The firefighters did their jobs as quickly as possible and made a hasty retreat. The following morning, the radiation levels at the plant dropped sufficiently for reinforcements to join the Fukushima 50, bringing the total number of workers on-site to 580.

"Little by little, in a small way, we started to have some hope," Takeyuki Inagaki remembers. "Up until then, we were spiraling further down . . . Now we were dangling there. We weren't falling anymore."

It might not sound like much, but after a week of ever-worsening conditions, they would take it.

On March 21, ten days after the earthquake and tsunami, power was restored to all six reactor buildings at Fukushima Daiichi. Although having electricity certainly made the work easier, the cooling systems that the operators had tried so desperately to keep working ten days earlier were no longer of any use. They were pumping thousands of tons of seawater a day into

Workers in radiation suits try to restore power to the units 3 and 4 reactors on March 18.

reactors 1, 2, and 3, where it flowed around the melted cores and pooled in a radioactive mess in the buildings' basements. It would be almost nine months before all three reactors reached cold shutdown.

The slow creep toward stability was difficult to see from outside the plant. In the first days following the earthquake and tsunami, refugees had been without power and access to outside news coverage. Even many of those who were forced to relocate when evacuation orders were issued were unaware of what was going on at Fukushima Daiichi during the crisis. But slowly, as power was restored in areas farther away from the plant, a steady stream of bad news came with it.

While many of the dire predictions that had been made about the crisis at the plant in the early days of the disaster hadn't come to pass, it quickly became clear that the three meltdowns had

had a devastating impact on the surrounding region, and would continue to do so for years to come.

On March 19, the Japanese health ministry reported that it had found radioactive iodine in cows' milk from farms in Fukushima prefecture. Two days later, on March 21, it found radioactive iodine and cesium on spinach harvested at farms up to 90 miles away from the plant, resulting in bans on the shipment of milk and produce from four nearby prefectures.

On March 24, Katsunobu Sakurai, the mayor of a town near the plant, recorded an impassioned plea for help and posted it on YouTube. Residents of the town, Minamisoma, had been in the 12- to 19-mile zone around the plant and had been told to stay indoors to avoid radiation. A full nine days after the order was issued, they were still trapped in their homes and evacuation centers, and they were running out of food. The order had forbidden people to travel into the area as well, so no deliveries would be coming. Sakurai feared they would starve.

Closer to the plant, the town of Futaba was eerily silent, its buildings frozen as they had been in the moments following the earthquake. Bookbags still hung on hooks in classrooms; dishes and pictures littered the floors of houses; signposts pitched at angles across streets. Instead of cleaning up the mess, 1,415 of the town's residents could be found more than 150 miles away, in a suburb of Tokyo. There, they had set up a town in exile at Saitama Kisai High School. Residents lived in classrooms or the school gym. Relief agencies served meals in the cafeteria. The school's administrative offices functioned as a makeshift town hall.

Eight years after the earthquake, a restaurant in Okuma could still be found exactly as it had been left when people evacuated ahead of the tsunami.

On May 11, they would finally be allowed to return to what was left of their homes and salvage important documents and keepsakes. Wearing radiation suits and able to take only what they could carry back with them on a bus, they had a scant two hours to sift through the wreckage and salvage what they could of their former lives.

More than 470,000 people on the Tohoku coast had been forced by the earthquake, tsunami, or nuclear disaster to leave their homes. Over the following year, many would return and rebuild. But the residents of Fukushima prefecture would be on the move for years to come.

lessons

Sociologists refer to the ways a culture remembers catastrophes like the tsunami as "disaster memory." In places where natural disasters frequently occur, disaster memory saves countless lives. Survivors tell their children and grandchildren about the events. The stories become local lore, which often carries vital lessons about what to do when disaster strikes again. But disaster memory isn't perfect. Over time, it fades. As decades pass without a major disaster, people begin to move back into the low-lying areas by the water. Fishermen want to be closer to their boats, builders want to take advantage of flat land near the shore, others just love the sea.

In Japan, memorial markers called "tsunami stones" remind the residents of many villages about the danger. A stone in the tiny village of Aneyoshi, in Iwate prefecture, sits at the high-water mark from a 1933 tsunami. It warns, "Do not build your homes below this point!"

In the village of Murohama, a shrine at the top of the town's largest hill carried a dire warning. When a tsunami swept through in the year 869, many of the village's residents had rushed to high ground there. But while the hilltop was high enough for them to stay dry when the first wave of the tsunami swept in from the sea, it was flooded when a second wave was funneled in over the land on the opposite side. Marking the place where the villa-gers were killed, the shrine alerted future generations to the false sense of safety offered by the hill. More than a thousand years later, villagers from Murohama knew to avoid the hilltop with the shrine and evacuated to a spot farther inland. From there, they watched as the shrine was swallowed by the tsunami.

Disaster memory spurs parents to teach their children about *tendenko*. It affects decisions about where to build houses and whether to build seawalls. It saved the village of Fudai. There, mayor Kotaku Wamura, who had seen the devastation caused by the 1933 tsunami, had insisted that the village's floodgate be 51 feet tall. When construction on the supersized gate began in 1972, many townspeople protested, calling it a waste of money. But Mayor Wamura, remembering the 1933 tsunami and sto-ries about the 1896 inundation, refused to budge. When the tsu-nami swept ashore in 2011, it brought a 66-foot wave to Fudai. But behind the floodgate, the village was safe. The massive wave overtopped the seawall but petered out after about 300 yards, long before it reached any buildings. Of all the villages on the Sanriku Coast, Fudai was the only one that remained intact.

But, while the morals of the stories told by tsunami stones and shrines are clear—don't build near the shore, run for high ground after an earthquake, always be prepared for the next tsunami—the lessons from the meltdowns at Fukushima Daiichi are much harder to pinpoint.

—∿—

In July 2017, more than six years after the disaster at Fukushima, a tiny robot swam through the unit 3 building. At less than 8 inches long, with a cheerful red cylindrical body, a saucer-shaped head, and four whirring propellers, the Mini-Manbo was decidedly cute. But the little robot was tougher than it seemed. Cleanup workers had been trying to get a look inside reactors 1, 2, and 3 for years. But the reactor buildings were filled with water and radioactive debris. Five robots that had tried to reach the reactor cores had been destroyed by radiation before they got there. Operators had finally managed to find the fuel in units 1 and 2, but unit 3, which was covered by more water than the other two, proved more difficult. The Mini-Manbo, which had special cladding to shield it from radiation and sensors that would allow it to avoid dangerous radiation hot spots, was the right robot for the job. After three days of picking its way around underwater obstacles, it was finally nearing its destination.

The Manbo's bright headlight cut through the pitch-black water of the flooded reactor building, recording a scene of jumbled metal and concrete. Flecks of debris floated in the soupy water, making it difficult to pick out shapes. Four operators steered the Manbo remotely, gathering critical information about the state of the reactor, until the robot finally found what it was looking for: the unit 3 reactor vessel. At its bottom, there was a giant hole where the melting fuel had eaten through the steel. Beneath that was a lumpy mass of cooled corium.

Although experts had long believed that the fuel in reactors 1, 2, and 3 had melted through the reactor vessels, it wasn't until this moment, more than six years after the meltdowns, that they had proof. The Mini-Manbo gave the final confirmation and pinpointed the location of the fuel inside the building. Armed with that knowledge, TEPCO could begin to make plans to disassemble the reactors.

Beyond the reactor building walls, things had reached a kind of normalcy, although it was a very different normal than it had been before the tsunami. Once again, the plant bustled with activity. About 7,000 workers reported to the complex every day. But now they spent their days planning and carrying out the monumental task of cleaning up a radioactive disaster zone. Plant workers and visitors no longer needed to wear full radiation suits when they entered the grounds. All of the soil on the site, full of radioactive dust, had been paved over to prevent it from becoming airborne. In order to accomplish that, all of the trees and other plants on the grounds had been cut down. Before the disaster, part of the complex had been a bird sanctuary, and 220 acres of forest had to be razed in the cleanup. Where grassy

Water storage tanks on the Fukushima Daiichi grounds in July 2018.

banks had once lined roadways, an unforgiving expanse of pale gray concrete now stretched as far as the eye could see. The trees and other plants—estimated to total almost 3 million cubic feet of radioactive litter—lay in massive brush piles on the plant grounds, held in place by heavy sheets of white plastic.

Closer to the reactor buildings, a thousand water storage tanks holding more than 250,000 gallons of radioactive water crowded the grounds. The frantic days of desperately trying to get water into the reactors had been replaced by a constant struggle to pump water out of them. Water was still being cycled through to keep the fuel cool, but groundwater also seeped into the buildings. If left alone, the groundwater would continue to flow toward the sea, carrying radioactive isotopes from the reactors with it, so workers pumped hundreds of gallons of water from the reactor basements every day. Although a decontamination process could remove some of the radioactive isotopes from the water, it couldn't clean all of it, so most of the wastewater was stored in tanks. In 2013, about 300 tons of it was accidentally dumped into the ocean.

Engineers had built an underground ice wall around the plant in 2016. Nearly a mile long, it was made of pipes that carried a super-cooling liquid to 100 feet below ground. The cold pipes chilled the surrounding soil, creating a barrier that would stop ground-water seeping in from the west. They also drilled wells to pump groundwater out of the ground before it could reach the reactors. But even with those safety measures in place, the amount of water being stored at Fukushima Daiichi would balloon to more than 320 million gallons by 2020. More than 75 percent of that stored water still carried more radioactive isotopes than the Japanese government considered safe, and the need for water storage continued to grow.

There was no place for the contaminated water that had already been stored to go. In fact, there was no place for any of the radioactive debris that had been bagged or boxed. Like many countries, including the United States, Japan lacks a safe nuclear waste storage system.

By 2020, the reactors themselves looked very different than they had when the accident occurred. Workers were constructing a strong shell around unit 1. The unit 3 building was covered by a giant barrel-shaped cap. And unit 4 was hidden beneath a sleek gray-and-white frame, built to unload fuel from its storage pools. All of the new structures were designed to catch any radioactive debris that might be knocked loose as workers dismantled the crippled reactors and moved fuel from their storage pools to a safer location.

The extra measures were essential to keeping workers and the people of Japan safe, but they made the work of cleaning up the mess much more difficult. TEPCO estimates that it will take as long as forty years to fully dismantle the reactors at Fukushima Daiichi. Where the radioactive pieces of the plant will go after the cleanup, and what will happen to the towns and villages nearby, is still unclear.

Several miles from the plant, the towns of Okuma and Futaba are still largely empty. For years, they fell within the Fukushima exclusion zone, an area that was too radioactive for the residents to return. The iodine 131 that spread across the area during the accident had a half-life of eight days, and it has largely decayed into safer elements; but cesium 137, with a thirty-year half-life, and Strontium 90, with a twenty-eight-year half-life, will likely take hundreds of years to completely decay.

Rather than wait, the Japanese government undertook a massive clean up, digging up radioactive soil from contaminated towns and hauling it away.

Radioactive debris is stored in plastic bags in the town of Naraha, which falls in the exclusion zone around the Fukushima Daiichi plant.

Scattered around Fukushima Prefecture, 721 dumpsites are filled with mounds of black plastic. From a distance, these piles look like heaps of regular garbage bags. But the gigantic heavy-duty bags—each able to hold about a ton of trash—are packed full of radioactive debris. The government has yet to find a place to permanently store the soil it has scraped from the towns of

Fukushima and until they do, the radioactive waste will continue to be a hazard. When a typhoon caused major flooding in the area in October 2019, hundreds of bags were swept into a river.

—∿—

In the years following the meltdown, organizations around the world, from the Atomic Energy Society of Japan to the International Atomic Energy Agency and the United States' National Institutes of Health, investigated the Fukushima Daiichi accident and attempted to explain its cause. As the reactors were melting down, it had been nearly impossible to keep track of what was happening inside them—operators couldn't even be certain units 1, 2, and 3 had all melted down until the Mini-Manbo found the last piece of evidence. Investigators sifted through radiation readings and TEPCO reports, scrutinized meeting transcripts, and gathered seismic and radiation data. Most agreed that the massive waves that had knocked out the power at Fukushima Daiichi should have been anticipated. But it was clear that TEPCO, in building the plant, had not planned for a tsunami of that size. Instead, it had built its plant to meet the minimum standards required by law. Even worse, when it built the plant in the 1960s, the company had actually lowered the hillside by more than 100 feet, digging out soil to bring the reactors closer to the water. Had the plant been built on the hillside at its original height, the reactors would have been out of reach of the tsunami. Insufficient government regulation had made it easy for the company to build a plant that was vulnerable to disaster.

But there were also things that went right at the plant. Although the fuel in the storage pools in the reactor buildings had become dangerously hot during the long ordeal, another onsite storage system had come through with flying colors. Before the tsunami, 408 spent fuel assemblies had been packed into cement casks on the plant grounds, in what is known as dry cask storage. Although they were rolled by the waves, the casks remained intact, and the fuel inside was untouched. It was clear to investigators that dry cask storage was a safer alternative to fuel pools.

But many of these lessons were lost in a larger question for which there was no easy answer: Is *any* nuclear power safe?

There's something about radiation that makes it uniquely terrifying. A lot of that probably has to do with its invisibility. Dangerous radiation can't be seen, felt, smelled, or heard, making it a particularly creepy hazard. And Japan, the only country to have been bombed with atomic weapons, has a particularly

The Daiichi disaster turned many Japanese citizens against the use of nuclear power. Here, people protest in Tokyo on June 11, 2011.

complicated relationship with radiation. In the months that followed the Fukushima Daiichi meltdown, when other reactors around Japan went offline for maintenance, the government withheld approval for them to reactivate. By May of 2012, all fifty working nuclear reactors in Japan had ground to a halt.

Japan wasn't alone in reconsidering nuclear power. A year earlier, the chancellor of Germany, Angela Merkel, had announced that eight German nuclear power plants would close. She promised to close nine more by 2022—making Germany a country without any nuclear power. Other countries followed suit.

On first look, this seems to make sense. The downsides of nuclear power are obvious when you consider Fukushima prefecture. Fallout from the meltdowns will affect the region for decades, possibly centuries. Once-green towns were scraped bare of vegetation and topsoil. In Iitate, the town with the highest levels of contamination, the cleanup cost came to about $1.8 million per household—and that didn't include the surrounding forests, which were impossible to clean. In the waters next to the plant, radioactive cesium settled on the seafloor and continues to be found in fish today. Radioactivity from the accident can be found in trace amounts as far away as California and Oregon.

The necessity of evacuating residents during the meltdown prevented rescue efforts after the earthquake and tsunami in nearby towns, and it also has been blamed for hundreds of deaths as the sick and elderly were uprooted—or left to fend for themselves.

But despite the real and devastating effects of the meltdown, forms of power other than nuclear fission may pose a greater threat to Japan. Since 2011, the country has focused on using other fuels to generate electricity, including coal and natural gas. By 2015, nuclear power provided just 1.5 percent of the energy in the country, down from about 30 percent before the earthquake. About ninety coal-burning plants accounted for 32.3 percent of the country's power, and the country had committed to adding thirty more.

Nuclear accidents can spread radioactive cesium, iodine, and strontium into the surrounding environment. But a properly functioning coal-burning plant spreads radioactive lead, uranium, radon, polonium, and thorium every day. These naturally occurring radioactive isotopes are found in the coal that is burned to make electricity. They become concentrated in fly ash, some of which escapes through the chimneys of coal-burning plants. Even worse, burning coal produces air pollutants, including sulfur dioxide and nitrogen oxide, that are real threats to human health. In a study commissioned by the environmental group Greenpeace in 2016, plans for new coal-burning plants on the outskirts of two major Japanese cities, Tokyo and Osaka, were estimated to have the potential to cause as many as 26,000 premature deaths over a forty-year period.

Coal plants are also a major producer of carbon dioxide, a greenhouse gas that contributes to global climate change. As an island nation with more than 18,000 miles of coastline, sea-level rise as a result of climate change is a very real threat to Japan.

—⁓—

It remains unclear how many people will suffer long-term effects from radiation exposure as a result of the Fukushima meltdowns.

A month after the tsunami, the accident was rated a 7 on the INES scale—a score shared with only the Chernobyl disaster. But the impacts of the Fukushima meltdowns were far less severe than Chernobyl's. At Chernobyl, the nuclear reactor actually exploded, spewing material from the reactor's core straight into the atmosphere. At Fukushima, while radiation did escape from the reactor vessels, the protective shells around the reactors remained intact. In the end, about ten times more radiation escaped at Chernobyl.

There have not been any cases of cancer linked to exposure among the workers who fought to prevent the meltdowns in the days following the tsunami. Fukushima plant superintendent Masao Yoshida did die in 2013 as a result of esophageal cancer, but because it was diagnosed quite soon after the accident (cancers take years, and even decades to develop) it was not believed to have been caused by the meltdowns. But a lawsuit brought by more than four hundred sailors who were aboard the USS *Ronald Reagan* during the disaster alleged that they had developed cancer and other ailments as a result of their exposure. A Japanese worker who participated in cleanup efforts at the plant starting in 2012 received workman's compensation for cancer as well, and in 2018, another cleanup worker died of lung cancer that was attributed to his work at the plant after the disaster. But the World Health Organization (WHO) concluded that, although there might be a very small increase in cancer risk for babies and children in the worst-affected areas, there would likely be no effect on residents elsewhere in Japan. And the United Nations Scientific Committee on the Effects of Atomic Radiation (UNSCEAR) found that the amount of radiation exposure as a result of the accident was too low to cause cancers in anyone outside the plant.

By far the greatest damage to the workers who weathered the days and weeks of stress at the plant was done by posttraumatic stress disorder (PTSD). In a country where people identify closely with their work, the emotional fallout from the accident was enormous. Despite their heroic efforts to save the plant, many of the Fukushima 50 felt personally responsible for the meltdown. Public anger at TEPCO spilled over onto its employees, and most of the Fukushima 50 chose to remain anonymous. Anxiety, depression, insomnia, and feelings of isolation were common in the workers, as well as in the former populations of the towns surrounding the plant.

Those towns are wildly different today than they were in 2011. In 2015, the evacuation order was lifted for the town of Naraha, about 9 miles from the plant. Two years later, residents were allowed to return to the towns of Namie and Iitate. About 40 percent of Okuma was opened up in 2019, as were about 1.5 square miles of Futaba in 2020. But residents have been slow to return. By 2018, only about 2,200 people had returned to Naraha, a town that had once had almost 8,000 residents. Two years after the evacuation order was lifted in Namie, about 1,000 people out of a former population of 21,000 had come back to their homes. Three hundred ninety-eight residents, out of the original population of 10,341, registered to return on the opening of Okuma, and fewer than 800 of the former population of 8,000 committed to return to Futaba. Of those who did move back, the majority were elderly.

The reasons so few came back are complicated. After living

elsewhere for years, many had put down roots in new towns. Children were attending schools; parents had found jobs. The population of Fukushima had already been declining for years before the accident, as residents left the rural setting for opportunities in cities. With the tsunami, the economy of Fukushima had come to a sudden halt, so there were few opportunities for work for former residents if they returned. But a lot of the evacuees were simply reluctant to come back to towns where pockets of radiation might remain. Many said they felt they had been misled by the Japanese government during the disaster, so they refused to trust the government's assurances that the towns were safe after the cleanup.

———⁓———

Outside the Fukushima cleanup zone, life has returned to the coastal towns of the Sanriku Coast. The rubble left by the tsunami has been cleared away, but the towns will never be the same as they were before the disaster. The Japanese government has been working to shore up tsunami defenses along the Tohoku coast. Forty-one-foot seawalls now line 245 miles of coastline. Many towns have enacted laws that prevent people from building on flatlands near the water.

Of those affected by the earthquake and tsunami, more than 47,000 people were still displaced from their homes nine years after the disaster. Most of those were from areas in the evacuation zone around the plant. But even for those who managed to return and rebuild, life is very different from the way it was before the crises. In all, close to 20,000 people died in the Great

Tohoku earthquake and the tsunami that followed. Family members and neighbors are gone, and many of the survivors are still dealing with the trauma of seeing their loved ones or homes carried away by the water.

As they have for millennia, the residents of Tohoku have worked to memorialize those they lost—to preserve their memories of loved ones and create lasting reminders of the tsunami for future generations.

The Okawa Elementary School, where so many students and teachers drowned, has been dug out of the mud and swept clean. Students now attend classes in a new building, but the original school still stands as a museum and memorial to the seventy-four students and ten teachers who died there.

New monuments dot the coast. In Natori, a sculpture marks the top of a hill where two hundred people, hoping to escape the tsunami, were killed. Shaped like a seedling to represent the town's determination to move forward, the sculpture is as tall as the wave that swept the townspeople away, serving as both a memorial and a warning to future residents.

In the town of Rikuzentakata, a single pine tree from a coastal forest of about seventy thousand trees survived the tsunami. But salt water had soaked its roots and eighteen months later, it died. The town preserved the nearly 90-foot-tall tree by creating an exact replica with a steel structure. The "miracle pine" stands today as a symbol of endurance and a reminder of the tsunami.

But one tribute seems to capture the pain of the tsunami victims and survivors more than any other. On a hillside behind Otsuchi, a telephone booth sits amid the long grass and flowers in a sunny garden overlooking the town. It's a cheerful white structure with a peaked roof, glass panels, and a sign that reads TELEPHONE OF THE WIND. Inside is an old-fashioned rotary phone that has played an unusual role in helping many move on after the disaster.

Its owner, Itaru Sasaki, is a retired fisherman who moved to this spot years ago because of its sweeping views of the sea. On March 11, 2011, he watched from his safe garden on the cliffs as that sea swallowed Otsuchi. In the days following the tsunami, he added the sign to the phone booth that sat in his garden. Survivors, desperate to say goodbye to those they'd lost, began to visit. They stepped inside the glass booth, picked up the receiver of the disconnected old phone, and began to talk to their missing loved ones. "If you tell yourself there's no sound," Sasaki says, "there won't be any sound. But if you listen very closely, you may be able to hear something."

In the six years after the tsunami, 25,000 people visited Sasaki's phone booth to leave messages for the dead. They were just some of the millions of Japanese citizens who had begun to find closure after the tsunami, to take the lessons of the disaster and move forward.

TIMELINE

March 11, 2011

P.M.   2:46   The Japan Trench ruptures

The Great Tohoku Earthquake begins

The tsunami is generated

3:27   The first wave of the tsunami reaches the Fukushima Daiichi power plant

3:36   The second wave of the tsunami knocks out backup generators in reactors 1, 2, and 4

9:00   The cooling water in the unit 1 reactor boils down below the tops of the fuel rods

9:00   The operators for unit 2 begin preparing to inject water into the reactor

9:23   The Japanese government orders residents within 3 kilometers (1.9 miles) of the plant to evacuate, and those within 3 to 10 kilometers (1.9 to 6.2 miles) to stay indoors

10:00   The unit 1 radiation level begins to climb

March 12

A.M.   12:34   (8:34 A.M. local time) The tsunami reaches Crescent City, California

2:00   The corium in reactor 1 melts through the bottom of the reactor vessel

4:00   Water injected into unit 1 using fire engines stops the corium before it melts through the primary containment chamber

5:44   The evacuation zone is expanded to a 10-kilometer (6.2-mile) radius of Fukushima

7:00	Prime minister Naoto Kan flies to Fukushima to meet with Masao Yoshida
9:00	The mission to vent unit 1 is aborted due to high radiation in the torus room
11:36	The RCIC system in reactor 3 stops working, and low water level triggers the HPCI system
P.M. 12:30	(3:30 P.M. local time) The tsunami reaches Antarctica
2:00	Operators use a compressor to open valves and vent unit 1
2:53	Unit 1 operators run out of fresh water
3:36	The unit 1 reactor building explodes, destroying power cables and injection hoses laid out for units 1 and 2
	The evacuation zone is expanded to 20 kilometers (12.4 miles)
7:00	Operators begin injecting seawater into unit 1

March 13

A.M.	The USS *Ronald Reagan* registers radiation on deck 100 miles from the coast and relocates
2:42	Operators shut down the HPCI in unit 3
2:45	Operators try but fail to open the steam release valves in unit 3
8:41	Venting begins in reactor 3
9:00	The water in unit 3 falls below the tops of the fuel rods
10:40	The unit 3 core begins to melt
P.M. 12:00	Hoses are set up to inject seawater into unit 2
1:00	A battery is hooked up to control panels to prepare for unit 2 injection/venting

March 14

A.M. 11:01	The unit 3 reactor building explodes, damaging hoses set up to vent unit 2

P.M. 12:00 The unit 2 water level begins to decline, and Yoshida orders injection of seawater

5:00 Water falls below the tops of the fuel rods in unit 2

6:00 Venting of unit 2 begins

7:20 The unit 2 core begins to melt

10:00 The drywell pressure soars in unit 2

March 15

A.M. 6:12 The unit 4 reactor building explodes

Operators hear that large explosion and notice a drop in pressure in the torus of unit 2; they assume the explosion happened there

11:00 Residents within a 20- to 30-kilometer (12.42- to 18.64-mile) radius of the plant are ordered to stay inside

Six hundred and fifty workers evacuate from Fukushima Daiichi; 70, who will become known as the Fukushima 50, stay behind

March 16

The U.S. ambassador to Japan, John V. Roos, recommends that all American citizens living within 50 miles of the plant evacuate

Helicopter check shows that there is water in the spent fuel pool at unit 4

March 17

Four military helicopters attempt to dump seawater into unit 3

March 18

Firefighters from Tokyo spray water into the spent fuel pools at unit 4 using high-pressure hoses

Radiation levels drop low enough to allow workers to return to the plant

March 19

The Japanese health ministry reports that it has found radioactive isotopes in cows' milk from Fukushima prefecture

March 21

Power is restored to all plant buildings

The Japanese health ministry bans the shipment of milk and produce from four prefectures near Fukushima Daiichi

2013

300 tons of radioactive water are accidentally released from storage at the plant.

2015

The evacuation order for Naraha is lifted

August 2016

Construction of the underground ice wall is completed

2017

The evacuation orders for Namie and Iitate are lifted

2019

The evacuation order for 40% of Okuma is lifted

2020

A small portion of Futaba is reopened.

GLOSSARY

asthenosphere: a layer of Earth's mantle that lies above the outer core and below the lithosphere; the rising and sinking of molten rock in the asthenosphere creates currents that move tectonic plates

atom: the most basic unit of an element; an atom is made up of a nucleus and the electrons that surround it

chain reaction: a chemical process in which a reaction creates by-products that, in turn, initiate further reactions

cold shutdown: in a nuclear reactor, the state in which the fuel's temperature is below the boiling point of water (212°F)

containment: in a nuclear power plant, structures surrounding the reactor vessel to prevent radioactive isotopes from escaping into the environment

core: the center of a nuclear reactor, where fission takes place; it includes the fuel rods, control rods, and water

corium: a lavalike substance that forms from the melted core during a meltdown; corium can be made up of fuel rods, structural steel, concrete, and other reactor materials in molten form

critical: a state in which a nuclear reactor is producing enough free neutrons to keep a chain reaction going but not so many that the reaction gets out of control

crust: a layer of the Earth made up of solid rock and minerals that, along with the uppermost mantle, makes up the outermost layer of the Earth (see lithosphere); there are two types of crust—oceanic crust (underlying the ocean basins) and continental crust (making up the continents)

decay heat: thermal energy that continues to be released by nuclear fuel after the reactor has been shut down

displacement: what happens when an object takes the place of water by pushing it out of the way

diverge: to move apart

dosimeter: a device that measures the amount of radiation absorbed over time

drywell: the open space that surrounds the reactor vessel within the primary containment

earthquake: tremors, resulting from a release of energy when a tectonic plate slips, that are felt on the Earth's surface

electrons: negatively charged particles that surround the nucleus of an atom

element: a chemical component that cannot be broken down into smaller parts through a chemical reaction; it is defined by its atomic number, which is the number of protons in its nucleus

epicenter: the point on Earth's surface directly above the point from which energy radiates during an earthquake

fission: the act of dividing something into parts; in nuclear fission, the nucleus of an atom is split into two pieces

friction: in physics, a force that resists objects' sliding over each other

Geiger-Müller counter: a device that measures the amount of radiation emitted by a radioactive substance at any given point in time

hypocenter: the place where a fault ruptures in an earthquake

ionizing radiation: radiation that is energetic enough to knock electrons out of an atom, creating ions

isolation condenser: a system that cools a nuclear reactor by running the steam it produces through a series of cooled pipes to condense back into water

kinetic energy: energy created by motion

liquefaction: the process by which soil or sand takes on the characteristics of a liquid

lithosphere: the solid outermost layer of the Earth, consisting of the uppermost mantle, oceanic crust, and continental crust, which is broken into tectonic plates

Love waves: seismic waves that travel along Earth's surface and vibrate in a side-to-side motion

magma: a hot, semi-liquid material found deep beneath Earth's surface; when cooled, it forms rock

mantle: a layer of the Earth between the crust and the core constituting most of Earth's volume; it includes the uppermost mantle (which also forms the base of the lithosphere), the asthenosphere (below the lithosphere and upon which the tectonic plates float), and the mesosphere (the thickest part of the mantle, lying below the asthenosphere and above the core)

megawatt: a unit of measure equal to 1 million watts; a watt is a measurement of energy released over time

molecule: two or more atoms that are bonded as the result of a chemical reaction

moment magnitude scale: an internationally recognized system for classifying the strength of an earthquake

neutrons: particles found in the nucleus of an atom that are neither positively nor negatively charged

nuclear boiling water reactor: a reactor that uses nuclear fission to produce steam used to generate electricity

nuclear fission: the act of splitting the nucleus of an atom into two parts

nucleus: of an atom, an area that lies at the center of the atom and contains the atom's most fundamental parts, neutrons and protons

potential energy: stored energy resulting from the position of an item

pressure: the force exerted against a container by molecules pushing against the surface

primary waves (P waves): seismic waves that travel through Earth's interior; they are able to pass through liquids

protons: positively charged particles found in the nucleus of an atom

radiation: energy that is emitted by an atom as particles break free during radioactive decay

radiation sickness: illness caused by exposure to large amounts of radiation

radioactive: the condition of emitting particles produced by nuclear fission or radioactive decay

radioactive decay: the process by which radioactive isotopes break down into more stable forms

radioactive isotope: a variation of an element that is unstable due to extra neutrons in its nucleus; radioactive isotopes emit radiation as they decay toward a more stable form

Rayleigh waves: seismic waves that travel along Earth's surface and produce a rolling motion

reactor: the part of a nuclear power plant where nuclear fission occurs

ria: an ocean inlet formed when a riverbed flooded

rotational energy: kinetic energy that is the result of an object turning around an axis (rotating)

scram: in a nuclear reactor, an emergency procedure that shuts down the reactor by stopping the chain reaction of fission

secondary waves (S waves): waves that travel through the solid and semi-solid layers of the Earth's interior but are stopped by liquids

seismic: having to do with vibrations in Earth's crust

seismology: the study of vibration in Earth's crust; the scientists who study this are called **seismologists**

shield: a physical object through which a certain type of radiation cannot pass; it protects anything behind it from that type of radiation

sievert (Sv): a unit of measure that indicates how much radiation an object has received

spent fuel: in a nuclear reactor, fuel that is no longer capable of maintaining a chain reaction

subduction: the process by which one tectonic plate is pushed underneath another

subduction fault: the area where one tectonic plate is being pushed underneath another

surface waves: seismic waves that travel along Earth's surface

tectonic plate: a massive chunk of Earth's surface made up of continental crust, oceanic crust, and uppermost mantle; it moves in response to the rising and sinking of the asthenosphere

tendenko: the traditional Japanese idea that residents of coastal areas should evacuate without delay before a tsunami arrives

thermal energy: a type of kinetic energy that is felt as heat

torus: also called a suppression pool or wet well; a doughnut-shaped chamber beneath a nuclear reactor vessel that is designed to contain and cool water during an emergency

tsunami: a massive wave of water produced by the displacement of a large amount of water, such as would happen during an earthquake or landslide

turbine: a piece of equipment that uses a force like wind or steam to rotate and produce power

unstable: a state in which conditions are likely to change; in physics, unstable elements are likely to decay or change form by some other means

valve: a device that controls the movement of a gas or a liquid into or out of a container

vent (verb): to release a gas or liquid from a container

BIBLIOGRAPHY

EARTHQUAKE AND TSUNAMI INFORMATION

Books

Birmingham, Lucy, and David McNeill. *Strong in the Rain*. New York: Palgrave Macmillan, 2012.

Independent Investigation Commission on the Fukushima Nuclear Accident. *The Fukushima Daiichi Nuclear Power Station Disaster: Investigating the Myth and Reality*. New York: Routledge, 2014.

Japan Center of Education for Journalist. *Life After the Tsunami, Volume 1: A Collection of the* Otsuchi Mirai Shimbun *News Reports*. Otsuchi, Japan: Otsuchi Mirai Shimbun, 2013.

Parry, Richard Lloyd. *Ghosts of the Tsunami*. New York: MCD/ Farrar, Straus & Giroux, 2017.

Rafferty, John P. (editor). *Plate Tectonics, Volcanoes, and Earthquakes*. New York: Britannica Educational Publishing, 2011.

Reports

Cosmo Energy Holdings Co., Ltd. "Overview of the Fire and Explosion at Chiba Refinery, the Cause of the Accident and the Action Plan to Prevent Recurrence." August 2, 2011. (press release)

Japan Meteorological Agency. "Lessons Learned from the Tsunami Disaster Caused by the 2011 Great East Japan Earthquake and

Improvements in JMA's Tsunami Warning System." Japan
Meteorological Agency, October 2013.

Pradel, Daniel, Joseph Wartman, and Binod Tiwari. "Failure of the
Fujinuma Dams During the 2011 Tohoku Earthquake." Paper
presented at Geo-Congress 2013, the American Society of Civil
Engineers.

UN Scientific Committee on the Effects of Atomic Radiation. *Levels
and Effects of Radiation Exposure Due to the Nuclear Accident
after the 2011 Great East-Japan Earthquake and Tsunami*. Report
to the United Nations General Assembly, 2014.

Articles

Buis, Alan. "Japan Quake May Have Shortened Earth Days, Moved
Axis." NASA.gov, March 14, 2011. nasa.gov/topics/earth/features
/japanquake/earth20110314.html.

Chang, Kenneth. "Quake Moves Japan Closer to U.S. and Alters
Earth's Spin." *The New York Times*, March 13, 2011.

Editors of *Encyclopaedia Britannica*. "Seismic Waves." *Encyclopaedia
Britannica*, August 10, 2012.

Fackler, Martin. "Powerful Quake and Tsunami Devastate Northern
Japan." *The New York Times*, March 11, 2011.

"Factbox: Japan's Many Earthquakes." Reuters, July 16, 2007.

FEMA Region IV Interagency Steering Committee. "A Federal
Perspective on Recent Earthquakes." *Partners in Preparedness*,
July 2011.

Fujinawa, Yukio, and Yoichi Noda. "Japan's Earthquake Early
Warning System on 11 March 2011: Performance, Shortcomings,
and Changes." *Earthquake Spectra*, vol. 29, no. S1, March 2013.

Ishigaki, Akemi, Hikari Higashi, Takako Sakamoto, and Shigeki

Shibahara. "The Great East-Japan Earthquake and Devastating Tsunami: An Update and Lessons for the Past Great Earthquakes in Japan since 1923." *Tohoku Journal of Experimental Medicine*, vol. 229, no. 4, 2013.

McCurry, Justin. "Japanese 'Miracle' Pine Returns to Tsunami-Hit Town." *The Guardian*, July 3, 2013.

National Oceanic and Atmospheric Administration. "March 11, 2011 Japan Earthquake and Tsunami." March 2015. ftp://ftp.ngdc.noaa.gov/hazards/publications/2011_0311.pdf.

Pletcher, Kenneth, and John P. Rafferty. "Japan Earthquake and Tsunami of 2011." *Encyclopaedia Britannica*, March 4, 2019. britannica.com/event/Japan-earthquake-and-tsunami-of-2011.

Powell, Devin. "Japan Quake Epicenter Was in Unexpected Location." Wired.com, March 17, 2011. wired.com/2011/03/japan-earthquake-surpise.

Schulz, Kathryn. "The Really Big One." *The New Yorker*, July 20, 2015.

Ujiie, Kohtaro, Hanae Tanaka, Tsubasa Saito, et al. "Low Coseismic Shear Stress on the Tohoku-Oki Megathrust Determined from Laboratory Experiments." *Science*, vol. 342, no. 6163, December 6, 2013.

U.S. Geological Survey Earthquake Hazards Program. "Earthquake Summary Map: The M9.0 Great Tohoku Earthquake (Northeast Honshu, Japan) of March 11, 2011." March 14, 2011. ftp://hazards.cr.usgs.gov/maps/sigeqs/20110311/20110311.pdf.

U.S. Geological Survey. "Kobe Earthquake Was Deadliest, But Not Largest In '95." February 23, 1996. (press release)

Yamaguchi, A., T. Mori, M. Kazama, and N. Yoshida. "Liquefaction in Tohoku District During the 2011 Off the Pacific Coast of

Tohoku Earthquake." *Soils and Foundations*, vol. 52, no. 5, December 27, 2012.

Zielinski, Sarah. "Fault That Caused Japan's 2011 Earthquake Is Thin and Slippery." *Smithsonian Magazine*, December 5, 2013. smithsonianmag.com/science-nature/fault-that-caused-japans-2011 -earthquake-is-thin-and-slippery-180948057.

Online Resources

Burgess, Joe, Jonathan Corum, Amanda Cox, et al. "How Shifting Plates Caused the Earthquake and Tsunami in Japan." *The New York Times*, archive.nytimes.com/www.nytimes.com/interactive /2011/03/11/world/asia/maps-of-earthquake-and-tsunami-damage -in-japan.html.

Incorporated Research Institutions for Seismology, "How Often Do Earthquakes Occur?" https://www.iris.edu/hq/inclass/fact-sheet/ how_often_do_earthquakes_occur.

NASA Science. "Solar System Exploration: Earth." solarsystem.nasa .gov/planets/earth/by-the-numbers.

National Centers for Environmental Information. "Great Tohoku, Japan Earthquake and Tsunami, 11 March 2011." ngdc.noaa.gov /hazard/11mar2011.html.

———. "Tsunami Data and Information." ngdc.noaa.gov/hazard/tsu .shtml.

National Hurricane Center and Central Pacific Hurricane Center. "Storm Surge Overview." nhc.noaa.gov/surge.

National Weather Service. "Flood Safety Tips and Resources." weather .gov/safety/flood.

NOAA Center for Tsunami Research. "Tsunami Forecasting." nctr .pmel.noaa.gov/tsunami-forecast.html.

U.S. Geological Survey Earthquake Hazards Program. "M 9.1-2011
Great Tohoku Earthquake, Japan." earthquake.usgs.gov/earthquakes
/eventpage/official20110311054624120_30/executive.

Weather Underground. "Historical Weather" (database). wunderground
.com/history.

Williams, David R. "Planetary Fact Sheets." National Space Science
Data Coordinated Archive, NASA. nssdc.gsfc.nasa.gov/planetary
/planetfact.html.

Videos

Clancy688. "Tsunami in Kesennuma City, Ascending the Okawa
River." 25:48 minutes. YouTube, April 8, 2013. youtube.com
/watch?v=P8qFi74k2UE.

Funahashi, Atsushi, director. *Nuclear Nation*. 96 minutes. Big River
Films, October 13, 2012.

Kooi, Brent. "Japan Earthquake—Liquefaction in Makuhari."
3:07 minutes. YouTube, March 26, 2011. youtube.com/watch?
v=rn3oAvmZY8k.

NUCLEAR FISSION AND FUKUSHIMA DAIICHI INFORMATION

Books

Atomic Energy Society of Japan Investigation Committee.
*The Fukushima Daiichi Nuclear Accident: Final Report of
the AESJ Investigation Committee*. New York: Springer,
2014.

Gale, Robert Peter, and Eric Lax. *Radiation: What It Is, What You
Need to Know*. New York: Alfred A. Knopf, 2013.

Independent Investigation Commission of the Fukushima Nuclear

Accident. *The Fukushima Daiichi Nuclear Power Station Disaster: Investigating the Myth and Reality.* New York: Routledge, 2014.

Lochbaum, David, Edwin Lyman, Susan Q. Stranahan, and the Union of Concerned Scientists. *Fukushima: The Story of a Nuclear Disaster.* New York: The New Press, 2014.

Mahaffey, James A. *Nuclear Power: Nuclear Fission Reactors.* New York: Facts on File, 2011.

———. *Nuclear Power: Radiation.* New York: Facts on File, 2011.

Reports

International Atomic Energy Agency. *The Fukushima Daiichi Accident: Technical Volume 1/5: Description and Context of the Accident.* Vienna, Austria: International Atomic Energy Agency, 2015.

Myllyvirta, Lauri. *Air Quality and Health Impacts of New Coal-Fired Power Plants in the Tokyo-Chiba and Osaka-Hyogo Regions.* Greenpeace International, May 2016.

National Research Council. *Lessons Learned from the Fukushima Nuclear Accident for Improving Safety and Security of U.S. Nuclear Plants.* Washington, D.C.: The National Academies Press, 2014.

Tokyo Electric Power Company. "Appendix: Voices of Field Workers." *Measures Taken at Fukushima Daiichi Nuclear Power Station and Fukushima Daini Nuclear Power Station.* Tokyo: Tokyo Electric Power Company, December 2011.

World Health Organization. *Health Risk Assessment from the Nuclear Accident After the 2011 Great East Japan Earthquake and Tsunami, Based on a Preliminary Dose Estimation.* Geneva, Switzerland: World Health Organization, 2013.

World Health Organization, Regional Office for the Western Pacific. *The Great East Japan Earthquake: A Story of a Devastating*

Natural Disaster, a Tale of Human Compassion. Manila, Philippines: World Health Organization , 2012.

Articles

Adalja, Amesh A., Eric S. Toner, Anita Cicero, Joseph Fitzgerald, and Thomas V. Inglesby. "Radiation at Fukushima: Basic Issues and Concepts." *Clinician's Biosecurity News*, March 31, 2011.

Associated Press. "Fukushima: Japan Ends Evacuation of Naraha as 'Radiation at Safe Level.'" *The Guardian*, September 5, 2015.

Batty, David. "Japan Shuts Down Last Working Nuclear Reactor." *The Guardian*, May 5, 2012.

Breidthardt, Annika. "German Government Wants Nuclear Exit by 2022 at Latest." Reuters.com, May 31, 2011.

Broad, William J. "Scientists Project Path of Radiation Plume." *The New York Times*, March 16, 2011.

Broad, William J., and Hiroko Tabuchi. "In Fuel-Cooling Pools, a Danger for the Longer Term." *The New York Times*, March 15, 2011.

Clegg, Brian. "20 Amazing Facts About the Human Body." *The Guardian*, January 26, 2013.

CNN Wire Staff. "WHO: Radiation in Japan Food 'More Serious' Than Thought." CNN.com, March 21, 2011.

de Freytas-Tamura, Kimiko. "Radioactive Boars in Fukushima Thwart Residents' Plans to Return Home." *The New York Times*, March 9, 2017.

Dvorak, Phred, Juro Osawa, and Yuka Hayashi. "Japanese Declare Crisis at Level of Chernobyl." *The Wall Street Journal*, April 12, 2011.

Editors of *Encyclopaedia Britannica*. "Fukushima Accident." *Encyclopaedia Britannica*, March 13, 2018.

Fackler, Martin. "Japanese City's Cry Resonates Around the World." *The New York Times*, April 6, 2011.

———. "Japan's $320 Million Gamble at Fukushima: An Underground Ice Wall." *The New York Times*, August 29, 2016.

———. "Radiation Fears and Distrust Push Thousands from Homes." *The New York Times*, March 17, 2011.

———. "Six Years After Fukushima, Robots Finally Find Reactors' Melted Uranium Fuel." *The New York Times*, November 19, 2017.

———. "Tsunami Warnings, Written in Stone." *The New York Times*, April 20, 2011.

Fackler, Martin, and Mark McDonald. "Need Overwhelms Japan After Quake and Tsunami." *The New York Times*, March 14, 2011.

———. "Death Toll Estimate in Japan Soars as Relief Efforts Intensify." *The New York Times*, March 13, 2011.

Goldenberg, Pippa. "How Many Atoms Does It Take for an Element to Become Visible to the Naked Eye?" *Jabberwacky*, March 13, 2015.

Grier, Peter. "Fukushima Nuclear Crisis: How Serious Is the Radiation Threat?" *Christian Science Monitor*, March 15, 2011.

Gross, Terry. "One Year Later, 'Inside Japan's Nuclear Meltdown.'" *Fresh Air*, National Public Radio, February 28, 2012. npr.org /2012/02/28/147559456/one-year-later-inside-japans-nuclear -meltdown.

Holguín-Veras, José. "Japan's 1,000-Year-Old Warning." *Los Angeles Times*, March 11, 2012.

Hong, B. D., and E. R. Slatick. "Carbon Dioxide Emission Factors for Coal." *Quarterly Coal Report, January-April 1994*. Washington, D.C.: Energy Information Administration, August 1994.

Hosaka, Tomoko A. "How One Japanese Village Defied the Tsunami." NBCNews.com, May 13, 2011.

Hurst, Daniel. "Town Where Nobody's Home: Fukushima Communities Struggling to Survive." *The Guardian*, March 8, 2018.

Imanaka, Tetsuji. "External dose assessment for inhabitants in Iitate village until evacuation after the Fukushima-1 NPP accident." *International Nuclear Information System*, Vienna: International Atomic Energy Association, 2014.

"Japan Earthquake: Anger Over Fukushima Evacuation Plan." BBC .com, March 16, 2011.

Kono, Etsuo. "Japan's Otsuchi 'Wind Phone' Lets the Living Talk to the Dead." *Financial Review*, August 18, 2017.

Levine, Gregg. "7 Years On, Sailors Exposed to Fukushima Radiation Seek Their Day in Court." *The Nation*, March 9, 2018.

Lim, Megumi. "Seven Years After Tsunami, Japanese Live Uneasily with Seawalls." Reuters, March 8, 2018.

Martin, Rachel. "Radiation Levels Force U.S. Ships to Change Course." *Morning Edition*, National Public Radio, March 16, 2011.

Matsuo, Icihro, "Contaminated Waste Bags Still at Risk of Loss in Fukushima." *The Asahi Shimbun*, March 18, 2020.

McCurry, Justin. "Fukushima 50: 'We Felt Like Kamikaze Pilots Ready to Sacrifice Everything.'" *The Guardian*, January 11, 2013.

———. "Fukushima Disaster: First Residents Return to Town Next to Nuclear Plant." *The Guardian*, April 10, 2019.

———. "Japan Lifts Evacuation Order for Town Hit by Fukushima Disaster." *The Guardian*, March 4, 2020.

McDonald, Mark, and Kevin Drew. "U.S. Urges Wider No-Go Area Around Nuclear Plant." *The New York Times*, March 16, 2011.

"Memorial Monuments in Sendai of the Great East Japan Earthquake." *Japan Info*, November 19, 2015.

Mori, Nobuhito, Tomoyuki Takahashi, Tomohiro Yasuda, and

Hideaki Yanagisawa. "Survey of 2011 Tohoku Earthquake Tsunami Inundation and Run-Up." *Geophysical Research Letters*, September 27, 2011.

"Nuclear Fugitives Return: The Struggle to Repopulate Fukushima." *The Economist*, May 26, 2017.

Osawa, Juro. "Elevated Radioactivity Found in Japanese Milk, Spinach." *The Wall Street Journal*, March 19, 2011.

Rich, Motoko. "In a First, Japan Says Fukushima Radiation Caused Worker's Cancer Death." *The New York Times*, September 5, 2018.

———. "Struggling with Japan's Nuclear Waste, Six Years After Disaster." *The New York Times*, March 11, 2017.

———. "The Children of Fukushima Return, Six Years After the Nuclear Disaster." *The New York Times*, April 21, 2017.

———. "The Lonely Towns of Fukushima." *The New York Times*, March 10, 2017.

Rich, Motoko, and Makiko Inoue. "Japan Wants to Dump Nuclear Plant's Tainted Water. Fishermen Fear the Worst." *The New York Times*, December 23, 2019.

Ryūshō, Kadota. "Homage to Yoshida Masao, the Man Who Saved Japan." Nippon.com, September 4, 2013.

Sanders, Katie, and Politifact. "Seven Years after the Fukushima Nuclear Disaster, Japanese Town Rebounds from Zero." *Tampa Bay Times*, March 8, 2018.

"Supermarket Opens in Namie for the First Time Since Fukushima Nuclear Disaster." *Japan Today,* July 15, 2019.

Tabuchi, Hiroko. "Masao Yoshida, Nuclear Engineer and Chief at Fukushima Plant, Dies at 58." *The New York Times*, July 9, 2013.

Tabuchi, Hiroko, David E. Sanger, and Keith Bradsher. "Japan Faces

Potential Nuclear Disaster as Radiation Levels Rise." *The New York Times*, March 14, 2011.

Tanaka, Chisato. "Japan Continues to Rely on Coal-Fired Plants Despite Global Criticism." *The Japan Times*, October 9, 2018.

"Town of Futaba Kicks Off Radiation Cleanup with Eye on 2022 Revival." *The Japan Times*, December 25, 2017.

"Tsunami-Hit Okawa Elementary Holds Ceremony Ahead of Closure in March." *The Japan Times*, February 24, 2018.

Wada, Koji, Toru Yoshikawa, Takeshi Hayashi, and Yoshiharu Aizawa. "Emergency Response Technical Work at Fukushima Dai-ichi Nuclear Power Plant: Occupational Health Challenges Posed by the Nuclear Disaster." *Occupational and Environmental Medicine*, vol. 69, no. 8, August 2012.

Wald, Matthew L. "Japan Orders Evacuation Near 2nd Nuclear Plant." *The New York Times*, March 11, 2011.

Watanabe, Yosuke. "47,000 People Still Displaced Nine Years after 3/11 Disaster." *The Asahi Shimbun*, March 11, 2020.

Watts, Jonathan, Tania Branigan, and Matthew Taylor. "Japanese Nuclear Plant Hit by Fire and Third Explosion." *The Guardian*, March 15, 2011.

Yoshida, Reiji, and Takahiro Fukada. "Fukushima Plant Site Originally Was a Hill Safe from Tsunami." *The Japan Times*, July 13, 2011.

"The Yoshida Testimony: The Fukushima Nuclear Accident as Told by Plant Manager Masao Yoshida." *The Asahi Shimbun*, December 3, 2014.

Zaveri, Mihir. "Fukushima's Nuclear Imprint Is Found in California Wine (Drinkers, Don't Panic)." *The New York Times*, July 20, 2018.

Videos

"Fukushima 360: Walk Through a Ghost Town in the Nuclear Disaster Zone." 3:09 minutes. *The Guardian*, March 11, 2018.

O'Brien, Miles. "Nuclear Meltdown Disaster." 54 minutes. *Nova*, season 42, episode 22, July 29, 2015.

Online resources

Department of Energy. "The DOE Ionizing Radiation Dosages Chart." https://www.energy.gov/sites/prod/files/2018/01/f46/doe-ionizing-radiation-dose-ranges-jan-2018.pdf.

Department of Energy. "How Does Radiation Affect Humans?" https://ehss.energy.gov/ohre/roadmap/achre/intro_9_5.html.

International Atomic Energy Agency. "International Nuclear and Radiological Event Scale (INES)." iaea.org/resources/databases/international-nuclear-and-radiological-event-scale.

———. "Fukushima Nuclear Accident Update Log." iaea.org/newscenter/news/fukushima-nuclear-accident-update-log-49.

Nuclear Energy Institute. "Fact Sheet: Comparing Fukushima and Chernobyl." nei.org/resources/fact-sheets/comparing-fukushima-and-chernobyl.

Nuclear Energy Institute. "Nuclear Fuel." nei.org/fundamentals/nuclear-fuel.

Tokyo Electric Power Company, "Inside Fukushima Daiichi." tepco.co.jp/en/insidefukushimadaiichi/index-e.html.

Tokyo Electric Power Company, "Treated Water Portal Site." tepco.co.jp/en/decommission/progress/watertreatment/index-e.html.

United States Navy. "Fact File: USS *Ronald Reagan* (CVN 76)." Naval Vessel Register, nvr.navy.mil/SHIPDETAILS/SHIPSDETAIL_CVN_76_5300.HTML.

QUOTATION AND SOURCE NOTES

Tsunami

Station Blackout

Meltdown

Lessons

ACKNOWLEDGMENTS

I didn't originally have plans to write a book about the meltdown at Fukushima Daiichi, but Simon Boughton, then publisher of Roaring Brook Press, suggested that I take it on. Once I started looking into the disaster, I was overwhelmed with curiosity. I live about 15 miles from the Indian Point Energy Center, a nuclear facility that, after the Fukushima quake, was revealed to be the one in the United States most vulnerable to damage from a seismic event. (While nuclear plants in California can be found close to much larger faults, they are earthquake reinforced. Indian Point, which is perched atop an older and far less powerful fault, is not. Indian Point also sits on the Hudson River, an estuary vulnerable to tsunami.) I jumped at the opportunity to learn more about nuclear power generation and its potential impact on the land around it. It's been nearly five years since that first conversation. Indian Point is now scheduled to be decommissioned in 2021. And researching and writing this book has filled a yawning gap in knowledge for me, for which I am truly grateful.

I was not far into that researching and writing before I realized the staggering complexity of the science behind the earthquake, tsunami, and meltdown in Fukushima. I am deeply indebted to the generous readers who reviewed the manuscript and gave me the benefit of their expertise.

Lita and Dave Judge were extraordinarily generous in

introducing me to Frederick S. Rogers, PhD, Professor of Geology and Environmental Science at Franklin Pierce University, who reviewed the information on the geology behind the Great Tohoku Earthquake and Tsunami. Eileen Shaughnessy Downey, PhD, Adjunct Professor of Chemistry at University of Richmond, was kind enough to offer her insights on chemistry. She is not only an intelligent and methodical reader but also the best stand partner a violinist could ever ask for. Isaac Langeland, Missile Technician First Class in the U.S. Navy, gave the benefit of his training in radiation protocols and shipboard mechanics. It's not every day that you get schooled on ionization by your little brother, so thank you for that. Jim Ottaviani, nuclear engineer and graphic novelist extraordinaire, set my mind at ease about my descriptions of the workings of a nuclear reactor. It turns out that he is not only a ridiculously talented graphic novelist with master's degrees in nuclear engineering AND library science—he's also a pretty fantastic editor.

Finishing drafts and editorial passes of this book meant a few too many late nights and unwashed dishes, so I owe major thanks (and apologies) to my husband, James Geppner, and especially my daughter, Freddie. They somehow manage to be supportive even when they're not getting enough cuddles.

And, of course, I owe huge thanks to Katherine Jacobs and Emily Feinberg, who took up the editorial reins of this book and saw it through to completion. Your patience knows no bounds. Thank you for wading into these murky waters with me.

IMAGE CREDITS

All maps, diagrams, charts, and infographics by Manuel Bortoletti.

INDEX

Page references in italic indicate a photograph; those with *f* denote figures, including maps, diagrams, charts, and infographics.